THE COSMIC WEB

THE
COSMIC
WEB

HOPE FOR OUR
WORLD THROUGH
SPIRITUALITY AND SCIENCE

JOY ANDREWS HAYTER, PhD

Foreword by
CYNTHIA BOURGEAULT, PhD

Red Elixir
Rhinebeck, New York

Paperback ISBN 978-1-960090-20-1
eBook ISBN 978-1-960090-21-8

Library of Congress Control Number 2023941639

Book design by Colin Rolfe
Cover art by Max Andrews, Ax Mandrews Design,
www.axmandrews.com

Red Elixir is an imprint of Monkfish Book Publishing Company

Red Elixir
22 East Market Street, Suite 304
Rhinebeck, New York 12572
(845) 876-4861
monkfishpublishing.com

To Ever Joy
The future of the world rests on pure hearts such as yours
Learn to keep letting go to the purity you are born with and always remember
that as you knock, as you ask, there is abundant help available

Contents

Out beyond ideas of wrongdoing and rightdoing,
there is a field.
I'll meet you there.

When the soul lies down in that grass, the world is too full to talk about.
Ideas, language, even the phrase 'each other' doesn't make any sense.[1]
—Jalal ad-Din Muhammad Balkhi (aka Rumi)

On that day you will realize that I am in my Father,
and you are in me, and I am in you.
—John 14:20 (NRSV)

Foreword
Cynthia Bourgeault, PhD

Science and religion have long since buried the hatchet (at least in the minds of most contemporary thinking people), but communication between them continues to be challenging. The problem is not a lack of good will, or of genuine curiosity to understand more of each others' domains. It's a translation problem between two very different methodologies and language styles. In religious discourse, words tend to be used metaphorically and associatively, with "correspondences" between items opening out into a field of broad new relationality. With this mode of inquiry, it's all about spotting unsuspected, connecting links and patterns largely in the connotative and image-attracting capacities of language. In science, words are used with much more precision and within specifically delimited domains. The attempt to meld hermeneutical styles can create a rigor that mystics find frustrating and a mélange of fuzzy associations that scientists find frustrating.

A cousin of mine, one of the early researchers in the field of elementary particles, always had a pet peeve with what he considered to be a completely airy-fairy appropriation of the Heisenberg principle by budding cosmic mystics, who transformed it from a specific principle pertaining to the wave nature of matter to a general statement about the relational nature of the universe. That widening gyre of metaphorical associations which is so energizing to religious consciousness, can seem maddeningly sloppy to a highly trained research scientist, particularly in those "esoteric" fields that religious/mystical types seem so drawn to: cosmology, astrophysics, and quantum physics. The tendency to reduce to the lowest and broadest common denominator then set it loose on extravagant metaphoric flights of fancy; this is, to almost every well-trained scientist I know, like fingers scraping on a blackboard.

Further aggravating this communications gap is the fact that so many of us "spiritual types" drawn to religious vocational pathways chose that fork-in-the-road early in our lives—certainly by college, for many by high school. I am a flagrant example here; as I try to delve into contemporary "quantum metaphysical" conversations with my high school chemistry and physics, I am obviously dependent upon translators—and how am I to assess which ones are reliable? Popular translations are all too often simplistic, vague, and naïve—not only scientifically but theologically, eliciting a similar "fingernails on the blackboard" response from those rigorously trained in traditional theo-logical and philosophical hermeneutics.

That is why I am so pleased now to introduce to you the work of Joy Andrews Hayter. Joy is a reliable bridgebuilder who can handle both disciplines (with their very different communication styles) with some-thing approaching a harmonious synthesis. While I first met Joy wear-ing her "religion" hat—as a spiritual director and respected spiritual writer and editor— I was soon to make the happy discovery that her background in science was equal to if not more extensive than in the liberal arts, and she could navigate both seas with an elegant simplicity.

Unlike some of us more "contemplative" types, who can wander for hours along the byways of mystical speculation, Joy has a practical "so what—how does this knowledge affect how I actually live my life?" attitude—that makes this book a breath of fresh air. She interprets the Christian Wisdom path well and deftly weaves in concrete examples and practical applications that put legs on the concepts all too often resisted as "too esoteric": she walks them straight into daily life. I con-sider myself well interpreted and respectfully transmitted here, and I am overjoyed that her clear, practical voice will allow these teachings access to a much wider audience, and in ways that they can be heard and acted upon.

Returning to my opening reflection on communication challenges, I would say in a broader way that this problem is not limited to the conversation between religion and science. So many of our areas of knowledge have become overspecialized and over-jargonized, accessible only to those speaking the same language—that the universal call for conscience and common action all too often gets tragically blunted. Every effort to build a two-way bridge of communication between parties who formerly couldn't quite "get" each other is not simply a gift to scholarship but a gift to the human spirit. I am honored that Joy has this talent, and that she has been so willing to share it. Dive into this gem of a book with my confidence and blessing!

Author's Introduction

Religion and science clearly represent, on the mental plane, two different meridians that it would be wrong not to separate.... But these meridians must necessarily meet at some pole of common vision (coherence): otherwise, everything in our field of thought and knowledge would collapse.

—**Pierre Teilhard de Chardin, in** *The Heart of the Matter*

Whenever the essential nature of things is analyzed by the intellect, it must seem absurd or paradoxical. This has always been recognized by the mystics, but has become a problem in science only recently.

—**Fritjof Capra, in** *The Tao of Physics*

This book was inspired by many people: some who have taught me science, and others who have taught me Wisdom. Some are embodied, and some are not. In its current form, this book was deeply inspired by Episcopal priest and mystic Cynthia Bourgeault. As I listened to her incisive talks on the Christian Wisdom tradition, riddled with references to modern science, I sensed an invitation. In response to her fluid references to quantum fields, coherence, energy, and the beauty implanted in matter, I found myself scribbling in the margins of my notes about the physics. I wanted to expand on the science and the beauty that I see shimmering through it, weaving the physics among her ideas on Wisdom. The synergy of the two seemed just too important to let go, and is so relevant for our world in its intense search for meaning, and even redefinition, on so many levels. At one point, Cynthia and I considered a short book on the two streams (that may yet happen), but meanwhile I've prepared this offering with her blessing (and occasional backstopping)!

There has been a recurring nudge throughout my life in the directions of both science and spirituality and a curiosity as to how they might come together. One of my influences in wanting to understand more about the spiritual implications of the physical world was Fritjof Capra's *The Tao of Physics*.[2] In the mid-1970s, Capra proposed that the relatively new science of quantum mechanics developed in the 1920s and 30s was related to principles of spirituality that had been part of human culture for millennia.

I felt excitement when I first read his book—it stimulated a deep curiosity and a sense of possibility that we may indeed be deeply interconnected in a relational reality. I wanted to know more. A seed was sown inside me, in a way my own "Tao of Physics" life experiment, that eventually drew me into a PhD program in physical chemistry and an immersion in contemplative practices. I wanted to get a sense for the truth in the scientific foundation for Capra's claims, and I wanted to experience the spiritual side, to see for myself whether they seemed to be connected.

Drawn to integrate science and spirituality

As a child, I was hungry to understand the world around me. I read nearly every book in the house, including an entire collection on Edgar Cayce (also called "the sleeping prophet"). The core of his teaching drew me in like a magnet: meditation and dream work. I was drawn to these two practices, intuiting that they held a key importance to an expanse of life, the universe and everything; to more dimensions of who we are. The two practices are complementary. In Tibetan Dzogchen teachings, for example, both waking life and dream are subject to our illusions, driven by our egoic desires and aversions. To break through into our true nature it is important to see through these illusions in both waking and dreaming life.

I was also drawn to go to church, without any adults. From about age eight on, I would take the hands of my two younger sisters and cross the four-laned Amsterdam Avenue in front of our apartment building in Harlem, and go to the Presbyterian church down the street. I was particularly drawn to a painting there, of Jesus knocking on a door. I later realized there was no handle on his side; the door could only be opened from within.

Despite the unusual points of view that I encountered, I was a scientist at the core: I wanted to understand how the world worked, and what made things happen. At about ten, I took apart the washing machine when it stopped working, poked around inside a bit and secured some connections, and put it back together—it worked! And when I later took up meditation in earnest I approached it, too, as an experiment, as a way of looking more deeply into things.

I first gave meditation a try as a teen, guided by a family friend. He was kind and generous with his time, taking me to meetings where we would sit on long benches and chant for a while, and then meditate quietly. To practice at home, I set up a short stool in my closet with a candle in front of me and sat quietly, hoping I wouldn't set anything on fire. Escaping to this tiny enclosure, I hoped to find peace, as well as something deeper: I sensed a potent mystery flowing beneath the stream of my life. I attempted to learn more about meditation from lessons sent to me in the mail, despairing at what they could possibly mean by gazing inward at my "third eye" as the instructions suggested. Sitting in the dark, looking gravely at the spot between my eyes,[3] I felt cross-eyed, frustrated, and silly. And I soon got distracted by boys, and the baffling world opening around me as I entered college. Decades later, my mother told me that at the ripe age of sixteen I told her I would teach meditation one day. Pretty brazen for such a failed meditator!

About fifteen years after that, married with two small children, I recalled my youthful hunger to grasp the mysteries of the universe (still retaining a naive surety that it was possible), and started a master's program in chemistry at California State University. In one of my courses, my ears perked awake when the professor started to talk about rules for the way matter was organized on a scale far below what we could normally see. The fluid, interactive shapes of the molecules that compose us were described by mathematical entities that sounded like music (spherical Bessel functions, harmonic oscillators, Hamiltonians). Some energy configurations were allowed but not others, making quantum leaps between them—much like the different vibrating shapes that sand leaps into on a drum as the pitch changes.

I was struck by this elegant order on a tiny scale underlying everything we are made of, and wondered why I hadn't noticed or encountered it quite like this before. I asked the professor what field of study this all came from and he said "quantum mechanics." As an undergraduate biochemistry major at Barnard College, I had learned some quantum mechanics as it applied to the bonds in chemistry, but it had seemed abstract and I was more interested then in partying. Now, I glimpsed a profound beauty that begged to be explored. Drawn in by this mysterious sub-nanoworld, I changed my major to physical chemistry with research in applied quantum mechanics and dove in with full force to probe the tiny-scaled physics underlying the amazing behavior of matter, the stuff of the world around us and in us.

Later as a professor at California State University, East Bay and a researcher at Stanford University's SLAC lab, I continued to probe these thresholds. Even as we used tools of X-ray physics to communicate with matter in its fundamental language, quantum mechanics, to study chemical transformations in the environment and in alternative energy materials, I held a deep curiosity about the foundations at the base of it all, on the quantum scale and below. I kept pulling relevant papers from the academic library to follow the rapid progress scientists were making. It was mind-blowing, and drew me deeper.

The spiritual side of my Tao of Physics life experiment also continued. When I completed the qualifying exams in my second year of the PhD program in chemistry at UC Berkeley I felt ready to indulge my fascination with the Nyingma Institute. I passed it daily walking down the hill after parking my car at Lawrence Berkeley Lab, its building surrounded by Tibetan flags in my favorite rainbow colors. One sunny January day, my feet turned and started walking towards it. I didn't see an entrance, just a long hedge. I tunneled through bushes to find a door—it turned out to be the back door. Encountering many pairs of shoes, I stepped over them and padded down the stairs. The man at the front desk looked startled at my unusual entrance, but in a friendly manner explained that they were offering classes exploring the spiritual aspects of questions raised by physics. My heart leapt out, to hear such alignment with what I was hoping for.

The person who had helped write the texts for the material that intrigued me at Nyingma, Steven Tainer,[4] was just starting to teach a class at a bookstore two blocks from my house across the bay. I signed up for his class instead—I could walk over after dinner and an evening with my kids! And I entered a wild inner journey that eventually brought me right back home; closer to the person I was created to be, and to an appreciation for a mysterious, creative presence in everyone, in everything; in all the cosmos.

My "extracurricular" Wisdom studies in graduate school came mainly out of Eastern traditions, merging threads from the Tibetan Buddhist Dzogchen tradition with Taoist yogic practices and Chan (a Chinese form of Zen) meditation practice. I loved that Steven's teaching began with the view that we didn't need to strive to become something else in order to please a being outside of ourselves. As a Wisdom teacher, he taught that we are whole from the very beginning. We just need to learn how to let go of the survival-based habits that we learned growing up, and let go to the completeness that has always been there. I learned to question and revisit the way I perceived myself, the world around me, and my relationship to it, in both waking and dreaming life. These experiences led me to get an inkling of a different kind of lived experience: more open and less defined by habits.

These were not theistic approaches but they were within the purview of perennial Wisdom, or *sophia perennis*, that underlies most of the world's major religions. They acknowledged a Source, a Ground of

Being at the heart of the cosmos. It was a relief to me to let go, at the time, of God language. That language for me was confused with my own childish interpretations of what God might be, conflated with my own sense of feeling judged—if I were good enough, only then would this old guy in the sky, somewhere up there outside of me, accept me, much less love me.

After years on this path, one afternoon on retreat in Sonoma County I woke from a nap in my Volkswagen "Vanagon" hearing a man's voice loudly declaring, "Feed my sheep!" I looked around in a daze—no one was anywhere near the van. I knew Jesus had said those words to his disciple Peter, but had no idea how it might apply to my life at the time. Still, spurred on by the discomfort of divorce and empty nest, within the next few years I found my way back to church and Christianity. I started doing contemplative practice with a group of people on Tuesday afternoons in the church, and soon found my way into Centering Prayer. This type of meditation was developed for the lay public by three Trappist monks: Thomas Keating, William Meninger, and Basil Pennington. Centering Prayer evolved from the Christian contemplative monastic lineage, in which echoes of the Christian Wisdom tradition still held forth. The practice involves letting go, over and over again, to the Source of our being, to Oneness, to God. The offering of Centering Prayer was a response to people calling for a contemplative practice within the church—people were hungry for it and going elsewhere, mostly to Eastern traditions, much as I had.

Then I encountered Cynthia Bourgeault, who considers Jesus a Wisdom teacher. Cynthia took the Wisdom tradition, which is beyond any particular religion and in fact lives outside of time as we usually consider it, and re-visioned it within the Christian context. I was delighted to find that she placed Centering Prayer within a more three-dimensional, integrated set of practices, much like the yogic Taoism I had studied. Her Wisdom School retreats included a careful balance of conscious work and prayer modeled on the Benedictine model (*ora et labora*), knowing that either of these alone is not enough to awaken a full human being. Her framework is also heavily influenced by the work of G.I. Gurdjieff, who emphasized awareness of what we are up to, inside and outwardly. Somewhat in parallel with the Buddhist schools that seek integration of body, energy and mind, Gurdjieff taught that we have three centers: intellectual, emotional, and moving, that must be in balance. Cynthia lays out the Wisdom framework in *The Wisdom Way of Knowing*, and her theology is summarized in *The Corner of Fourth and Nondual*. Her dazzling array of books include works on the Trinity, Mary Magdalene, and the Wisdom Jesus.

Cynthia's pioneering work on re-articulating the Christian Wisdom tradition also strives to place it directly in the context of twenty-first century science. Influenced by scientist-mystics including Pierre Teilhard de Chardin and Jacob Boehme, her talks are often peppered with scientific terms in layperson's language. Every time I heard her lay out these terms within the Wisdom context, the scientist in me felt inspired to express the magnificence and mystery that I see from the scientific point of view. A strong force kept driving me to write—there is something here that needs to be expressed!

Cynthia's retreats and writings have touched me deeply, slowly helping to expand my (often unconscious) view that contemplative practice is a self-improvement project to a sense that, wow, we are smack in the middle of a great cosmic unfolding and we have a part to play! Our world can use this kind of awakening, and I hope this book can be a part of that, to help you open to seeing the universe and our role in it in a new way. Her influence is throughout this book. She has coined unique phrases, such as the "egoic operating system" and the "red shift/blue shift" model. The discussions of the Divine Exchange are also highly influenced by her Wisdom School teachings. Her ideas (and some of her favorite quotes) deeply permeate the thoughts I present.

And so, the Tao of Physics life experiment continues. As a scientist and contemplative some things I've wondered are: What is this place? What can we say about its rules, and the mysterious, fluid, energetic structure that underlies all matter? Why aren't we usually aware of the mystery that is pulsing through it? What does it mean for us to be a part of the web of creation painted by physics and Wisdom, and how can we learn to participate more fully in it? What might that mean for our connection with each other and with our planet, and with where we are headed?

You are invited to come along and visit these questions for yourself as well.

Chapter 1

Science and Wisdom
A Conversation for Our Times

The most beautiful experience we can have is the mysterious.
It is the fundamental emotion that stands at the cradle
of true art and true science.

—Albert Einstein, in *The World as I See It*

Conditions in our world are allowing a conversation to take place between Wisdom and science. The renewal and spread of contemplative practices and the explosion of mind-blowing discoveries are drawing us deeper into the mysterious nature of reality. More than that, these two realms are speaking to each other, and what they are learning from each other helps us interpret each of them more clearly. There is a call and response. For those who are detecting the resonance it is not just a privilege to be alive at this time, but a responsibility. It is absolutely critical that this exchange take place.

The growing edges, the "thin spaces" of both spirituality/religion and science approach each other quite intimately. Current scientists are humbled by how much still remains unknown, or difficult to interpret. And at the contemplative edge of religion where the mystics hang out, people are scratching their heads and saying, this new physics reminds us a lot of what the mystics have been telling us all along. These two seemingly disparate paradigms are both pointing to the same thing: a hyper-connected, interrelated reality where far more is possible than usually meets the eye. This relational web runs deeply through all our interactions; our exchanges with the world and with each other. In any given moment we have access to a connected, powerful Wisdom spanning the entire cosmos; and we can learn to participate in a more complete, even joyous exchange with it.

This web of connection is crucial to acknowledge, especially now. Our world, and all the species on it including ourselves, are in a time of deep flux. Our global health and social structures are under such intense stress that what we do now and in the next few years will have an immense impact on the next generations and on the livability of our planet.

What can we do? So many of our spiritual companions, friends, fellow scientists, and participants in Wisdom circles and meditation teams keep asking this question. And we often find that we may be asking ourselves the wrong question. What we do is of course important, but even more important is how we *BE*, how we live, and what quality of being we bring to any situation. Whether we are sweeping the kitchen floor, or exchanging a hello with a janitor or other colleague, all the tiny things we do each day add up to a huge impact. If I am reaching to pull a piece of bread out of the bag but inwardly am grasping for the next moment and trying to push through this one as though it doesn't count, I'm, in a way, being disrespectful of the whole world. If I notice that I am doing this, and instead choose to fully occupy this moment and even my body as I do this—my day, and even the world, are going to be different; possibly rippled out to a degree I can't even fathom.

This concept might sound odd—our dominant culture encourages us to look at larger things and measure impact in terms of wealth, privilege or status. But we are all participants in a flowing, generative, and abundant web of being that underlies all that we do, all we encounter, and all that we fundamentally are. You may have noticed that the deeper you look into what you really are, and into the profundity of what is around you, the more an echo of this relational web reaches you. As Elizabeth Barrett Browning wrote in her poem "Aurora Leigh":

Earth's crammed with heaven,
And every common bush afire with God;
But only he who sees takes off his shoes;
The rest sit round and pluck blackberries.

We are invited to turn and see, much as Moses did (see Exodus 3:1-5) when he saw the bush that was burning but not consumed. He turned, saw, and appreciated the thinness of the veil in that place, and took off his shoes in reverence for the deep holiness he perceived. We are encouraged to be aware of what is around us and within us, to look more closely at what we don't understand, and to grow more comfortable with paradoxes and unknowing. We are invited to fully occupy our lives and find out what that might mean for us and for our world.

I hope that you will keep an open mind as I lay out layers in this book, science upon mystical, mystical upon science. Each helps clarify the other: the wisdom of mystics helps us interpret the meaning of the complex theories of modern physics, and physics helps us penetrate more deeply into the mystery described by contemplatives. If you consider yourself a spiritual seeker or practitioner, the gentle physics presented here may open your eyes and broaden your view. Perhaps it may change your sense of spirituality to see such magnificence, such wondrous burning bushes, written into the structure of everything that we are made out of; written into the cosmos.

I invite you to see how some of these scientific and spiritual wonders touch you. If some of it rings true, what might it mean for you? How might these lenses be applied in your life? In this moment?

Our world is depending on it.

Chapter 2

Bringing Our Spirituality into the 21st Century

On that day you will realize that I am in my Father, and you
are in me, and I am in you.
—**John 14:20 (NRSV)**

Jesus said these words to his disciples at their last meal together, before he was taken away by Roman soldiers in events that led to his death. His words point to a mysterious mutual indwelling of our being with the divine, and therefore with each other. Jesus was a Wisdom teacher,[5] urging those around him to awaken, to come to their full potential. He was teaching people how to transform their being from self-centered, rote thinking and behavior to genuine love and compassion. As with any Wisdom teacher, we can't really know the true meaning of his parables and teachings with our regular minds, our intellect alone. He told us that his teachings had meanings on several levels, often saying: "If anyone has ears to hear, let them hear." He also showed his disciples how to grow these ears to hear.

It's hard to relate to religion steeped in an outdated cosmology

Many of the world's major religions are at least subtly colored by the cosmology that was prevalent a couple of millennia ago: we live on a flat earth with a heavenly realm floating somewhere above it; a place where we might go when we die if we believe hard enough or follow the right rules or become enlightened enough. And this outdated cosmology continues to color the focus of much of modern religion, not just the more fundamentalist streams. Even as we acknowledge a spherical earth, we tend to view heaven, or any sense of the divine, as outside of ourselves.

Jesus' teachings on our humanness and potential for transformation are also usually interpreted within this outdated cosmology. In past centuries most Christians, except for the occasional mystics (who were often silenced), focused on learning about Jesus and the events in his life, but lost the emphasis he was teaching his disciples: *we live in a relational web of being.* When he said "love your neighbor as yourself" he literally meant for us to love our neighbor *as* ourselves, not *as much as* ourselves.[6] When we look at the New Testament writings in Aramaic, the language that Jesus spoke, the Aramaic word translated as "as" in this phrase means "as if," "even as," or "as though."[7] We are to love our neighbor as ourselves, intimately related in a web of "interbeing," as Buddhist teacher Thich Nhat Hanh called it. Christian mystic Thomas Merton wrote of a sense of this interbeing:

> In Louisville, at the corner of Fourth and Walnut, in the center of the shopping district, I was suddenly overwhelmed with the realization that I loved all these people, that they were mine and I theirs, that we could not be alien to one another even though we were total strangers. It was like waking from a dream of separateness, of spurious self-isolation. . .[8]

And there are echoes of modern physics within the experience of oneness that Merton described.

No separateness: A quantum field?

We are ordinary human beings, wending our way through life and making mistakes, large and small, all the time. But on that day for Merton, the veil to another way of being opened up for a moment. As he wrote a few sentences later, "the gate of heaven is everywhere."[9] The point of relaying his experience is not that there is something special about Merton, but to confirm your intuition, however quiet inside, that there is something special about *you*, and the way we are interconnected in the vast quantum field. His story is not about one person's special experience, but a story of everyone on that corner, and by extrapolation, every being. It is a story that is going on all the time in the midst of the ordinary. It is a story of something that permeates the ground of the cosmos, and of our being, the undergirding of what Jesus taught. It's like a gigantic Higgs field[10] of hyper-connection, that surrounds and includes all of us, permeating and underlying whatever might seem to be going on in any given moment. It can just be hard for us to see most of the time. And physicists also point to a mysterious world underlying reality as we generally experience it.

Everything is connected

The atoms or elementary particles themselves are not real; they form a world of potentialities or possibilities rather than one of things or facts.
—Werner Heisenberg

If you had a super-magnifying glass to look inside anything at the sub-atomic level—baseballs, our hands, sand, etc.— you would see that *nothing solid is really there!* Tucked into absolutely everything we encounter in our everyday world are atoms, most of them birthed from stars. These atoms can join in a dynamic dance to make molecules, and molecules join to make cells, organs, organisms, and universes. Yet the atoms themselves are mainly empty space, or at least not full of particles, in the usual sense we expect from our Newtonian point of view. On the quantum scale of the atom we find a tiny nucleus[11] surrounded by lots of space: the atom is a lot more like a field of potentiality than what we think of as actual hard matter. When we stand on the ground we don't fall through because the quantum clouds around the atoms in the ground meet the quantum clouds of the atoms in our feet—they repel each other sort of like the way the opposing poles of two magnets repel each other.

And when we turn to a scale far smaller than the atom, we meet an even stranger world. At the Planck scale,[12] matter is wildly free and resists capture by scientific instruments. This region lies entirely outside our spacetime continuum. Here we see a universe where everything is connected to everything else in an elegant, orderly mystery. We find a vibrating field where virtual particles glance into existence and then disappear, in a shimmering dynamism that stabilizes the entire universe.

Grounded spirituality does not have to negate modern science

The new physics paints a highly interrelated, even spiritually vibrant, cosmology. As physicist Sean Carroll said, "There is only one wave function, which describes the entire system we care about, all the way up to 'the wave function of the universe' if we're talking about the whole shebang."[13] Think about it as a huge trampoline: if you were to jump on one end of it, the whole thing would vibrate. It's all connected. Compared with classical Newtonian physics, where separate objects interact in predictable ways, this is a huge paradigm shift. And with this shift our views of life, relationships, and our role in the cosmos have a lot of catching up to do!

The dominant cosmology left over from Isaac Newton and others, that informs the way we go about our lives, relationships, plans, and even our religions, presumes a three-dimensional world that can be defined in a neat Cartesian grid. This paradigm is subtly colored by the view that, if we just knew all the conditions at the present, we could predict exactly where everything would end up. Or that we could know absolutely everything there is to know if we had the proper tools and enough time. The Newtonian cosmology also presumes a dualistic separation: me vs. you, here vs. there, up vs. down, now vs. later. But many physicists, and also mystics, embrace paradigms that are more open-ended and nondual, pointing to an interrelated and interdependent universe where separation makes far less sense.

We can begin to ponder the mysteries of theology within the context of the mysteries of science, where so many questions remain. For example, we can view Jesus' words from the lens of this relational field. We begin to see that what he says about a world of mutual indwelling sounds a lot like the quantum field of interbeing, of interconnection: what he teaches is in alignment with the current cosmological view.

It is not only about us

As Cynthia Bourgeault said in one of her Wisdom Schools, "When we follow a true wisdom teacher like Jesus, or 'put on the mind of Christ,' as St. Paul called it, we can awaken the faculties inherent in our humanness that allow us to experience this relational web, and live from it as responsible, awake human beings."[14] From the point of view of the web, our path is not about our own salvation or how we can personally become more perfect, but each person thrives within a vibrant whole; we get there together or not at all. This is echoed in the highest Buddhist teachings, e.g. of Dzogchen and other branches as well: in our core being we have never left the whole, yet a Bodhisattva is one who commits to continued work with humans, striving for the benefit and happiness of all beings until everyone realizes that they too are complete, and part of a synergistic whole.

We must reach out to each other as parts of one shared whole.

"Nothing exists by itself alone. We all belong to each other; we cannot cut reality into pieces. My happiness is your happiness; my suffering is your suffering. We heal and transform together," wrote the great Buddhist teacher Thich Nhat Hanh.

Wisdom teachings, as well as some of the best art, music, and other creative expressions remind us that we are not alone in this vast quantum web of being: there is an inherent Oneness in the reality we share, and in which we are intimately related and mutually responsible. A responsibility to our greater community becomes far more immediate than just a sense of justice that we *should* help others, or care for our planet. Helper vs. helped, healer vs. sufferer/healed are dual, Newtonian concepts. In a nondual relational reality, we find we *must* reach out to each other because we are part of a shared Oneness. And this Oneness is written into the fundamental structure of the universe, hidden in plain sight, almost like a secret code for us to find in our intimate, relational reality.

Wisdom in times of crisis

This book is emerging during the time of multiple global crises including climate change, the tail end of a pandemic, and massive social injustice. These types of crises evolve when we forget who we are: both personally and corporately, we tend to focus on short-term gains of self-interest. We forget that all we see and touch is intimately connected with everything else. Ecologists and people from many Indigenous cultures know this. But in forgetting this connection we often wreak havoc, in what we do or in what is done on our behalf, to maintain the lifestyle of privilege we have grown used to. It is not sustainable, and the breaking point is becoming apparent.

In the field of imaging, scientists use algorithms to analyze groups of pixels, determining where the edge of one material stops and another begins. There is a "waterfall algorithm," which pays attention to steep changes in the image to help find the most important edges and ignore tiny local changes within a material. This helps us find the true edge of an object, rather than local bumps and valleys. As a society we are in the center of one of these rapidly changing situations right now. It's not comfortable to be careening over the edge of a waterfall, but here we find ourselves.

This plunge can bring grief. Grief at the millions of acres that have been burning all around us, destroying and displacing people, animals, and habitats. At the loss of clean air. At the catastrophic events that used to occur once every few decades now occurring regularly and with increasing strength: extreme temperatures, powerful hurricanes and typhoons, floods, winds, and famines. At the horrible treatment of human beings, especially those who don't look like or think like, or don't have the financial resources of those who are in dominance. And grief that grasping for power or esteem, rather than human compassion, often drives our governments and their decisions about what to do with any of this. People, and our planet, are suffering.

However, rather than a cause for panic, these crises provide an opportunity to look into our roles as planetary citizens. As they continue to unfold there is a danger of becoming more fearful and xenophobic, rejecting those fleeing from unlivable conditions, or those who have less or appear different from us. We can turn a blind eye to these crises if we create mini-environments where we think we have everything we need, personally, to survive. But we don't thrive in this life alone. We are highly interdependent beings and have an opportunity, an obligation even, to bring forth another way of being into the center of this intense, unprecedented morass of events taking place. For example, we have vast knowledge of ways to harness the energy of the sun and other alternative sources that won't create greenhouse gases that are central to climate change. We know how to feed people, to be kind, to respect our fellow human beings, and to share what we have. We could put our resources into these instead of other resource-hogging systems such as multi-billion-dollar election campaigns and weapons of war, to name just two.

More importantly, we can contribute to a continuous renewal in our world by consciously bringing qualities of compassion, kindness, patience, love, joy, goodness, and self-control into the mix. In our highly interrelated cosmos, our authentic expression of these "fruits of the spirit" makes a huge difference, and even more so if we do it together in a coherent, aligned offering. In a relational field of being where "you are in me and I in you," our offering is crucial.

How do we do this in the midst of all that is going on? The contemplative practices and the science presented here can hopefully open our minds to the sense that we are indeed all interconnected: your suffering is my suffering and your joy is my joy. We *are* responsible to one another, and to our planet. And the more we learn about opening to the vast, interwoven luminous field that shines throughout the cosmos, the more we can become a light. Our smallest actions can shine and reverberate and effect powerful change starting from within, tapping into a great cosmic heart, honoring our ultimate connection.

This relational reality is beyond the grasp of our intellect or ordinary mind. Science tells us that reality is so odd that our normal thinking brain cannot comprehend it; it's not at all like what we usually perceive. Even the brilliant physicist Richard Feynman said before a lecture on light and matter: "It is my task to convince you *not* to turn away because you don't understand it. You see, my physics students don't understand it either. That is because *I* don't understand it. Nobody does."[15] So to be clear, we're opening up some physics in this book, but we're not aiming to understand it with our heads. We want to play with it, to hold some of it open in a friendly way, and begin to unpeel the congealed edges around our hearts, awakening the mystic within our being who can begin to sense its meaning for us.

Questions for reflection:

- What experiences have you had of feeling connected with another in spite of physical distance?
- When have you felt the intimate presence of a sense of being that extended far beyond yourself, or felt a loving divine presence within yourself?
- How does it feel in your body, and emotions, to ponder an intimate connection with the universe, and even a personal responsibility for co-creating a sustainable world? What questions arise for you?
- It may help to take a moment to jot down some of your thoughts and questions, as you integrate some of this newer challenging material.

Chapter 3

Seeing What is "Hidden in Plain Sight" Requires the Tools of Wisdom

When I use the term Wisdom, I am designating a precise and comprehensive science of spiritual transformation that has existed since the headwaters of the great world religions and is in fact their common ground. This science includes both theory and practice. The theory part consists of a unified cosmology—in other words, a comprehensive vision of our human purpose and destiny. The practice involves a systematic training for growing into that purpose.

—Cynthia Bourgeault

Wisdom way of knowing

Our intellect, often inspired by insight, is an important place to come from. Intellectual pursuits, for example, have fostered amazing scientific discoveries about what we are made of, and the universe in which we find ourselves. They have engendered an array of technological developments, and they inspire conversations about so much that is relevant to being a human being today. But the intellectual approach is not the only way for observing, processing, and expressing ourselves. A world where only the intellect dominates is comically incomplete, leaving out the heart of who we are.

In order to begin to make sense of the intriguing, mysterious picture that science is painting and what it means for us, it is helpful to look back at what the mystics have sensed and told us. More importantly, we need their ways of seeing, their prisms to reveal what is usually unseen: these ways, beyond the confines of any given religion, are called Wisdom.

Wisdom is a common ground underlying the contemplative side of many of the world's religions, including Buddhism, Islam (e.g. Sufism), Judaism (e.g. Kabbalah), and Christianity (e.g. the contemplative monastic lineage). In contrast to the aspects of religions that focus mainly on beliefs or certain rituals, Wisdom lays out a path for transformation of consciousness that tunnels to the heart. This different way of seeing is sometimes called "wisdom mind," "seeing with the heart," "Zen mind," or even a "primordial state of pure presence."[16] Outside the realm of our usual busy, grasping way of being, this way of seeing can bring awareness of dimensions beyond time and space—of no separation. This way of seeing and being may seem unfamiliar to us at first, and we can easily breeze right on past it. If we tried to find it, it might seem like nothing was there, certainly nothing worth "looking" at, from our usual point of view.

Let's look more deeply at one of the wisdom paths, the one closest to my own heart: the Christian Wisdom tradition.

Bringing the Christian Wisdom tradition back alive

Christianity isn't a failure; it just hasn't been tried yet.
—G.K. Chesterton

This is one of Cynthia Bourgeault's favorite quotes. She offers hope that Christianity need not die out as outdated; it just needs to be presented within a broader Wisdom framework that brings together a more integrated and embodied perspective. In *The Wisdom Way of Knowing* Bourgeault writes:

How could an ancient cosmology have anything to say to our modern world? That's the astonishing part: the Wisdom cosmology is bold, spacious, and remarkably contemporary. In fact—and this is what drew me to it in the first place—it contains some missing pieces that somehow fell out of our Western cultural worldview and are crucially needed as we grapple with the questions of our meaning and accountability in a fragile and overstressed world. There are pieces here that can break down the wall between science and religion, reconcile intellectual freedom with moral integrity, and provide an utterly compelling argument for our global ecological responsibility.[17]

The Wisdom way of knowing broadens our perspective to see our roles and responsibilities within an intricately relational reality. More spacious, accepting, and open, the Wisdom way of knowing is a type of perception that arises from a way of being that integrates our faculties. Buddhists sometimes call it integration of "body, energy, and mind," and G.I. Gurdjieff would call it "three-centered" awareness. Wisdom School students learn that Wisdom is not knowing more, it is knowing with *more of you*.

Being awake: Three-centered awareness

The integrated mind of Wisdom includes far more than our intellect alone. According to Gurdjieff, it incorporates three ways of knowing inside us: the intellectual center (the way our mind knows), the emotional center (that knows through empathy, intuition and the resonance of mirror neurons), and the movement center (that knows through exploring the world via sensation and rhythm). These centers don't move at the same pace: the wisdom of the body perceives more quickly than the intellect, and the emotional center processes even more quickly. Malcolm Gladwell implies these other ways of knowing in his book, *Blink*, when he talks about a sense of intuition that is essentially instantaneous and beyond our usual thought processes.

When talking about three-centered knowing, Gurdjieff pointed out that we tend to reside mainly in one center—the intellectual center, for many in our culture—but it could be any of the three. He called the partial consciousness of being in only one center "being asleep," vs. the state of being awake as consciously functioning in all three centers, grounded in the present. Other prophets and mystics have also used the analogy of sleeping or wakefulness: there are many sayings throughout sacred texts urging us to keep awake. Jesus urges people multiple times, "Stay awake."[18] Sufi poet Hafiz said, "An awake heart is like a sky that pours light." Many mystics, describing their experiences from an awakened state—the open, contemplative mind that is sometimes called "seeing from the heart"—have described the falling away of an isolated, localized self in a particular moment in time, to a sense of openness and Oneness.

Viewing with the tools of Wisdom helps us see a broader reality

> *It would be possible to describe everything scientifically, but*
> *it would make no sense: it would be without meaning, as if*
> *you described a Beethoven symphony as a variation of wave*
> *pressure.*[19]
>
> **—Albert Einstein**

In the awakened state we can become much more aware of the interconnected, inter-relational reality that underlies our being; that physics is gesturing towards. And we have the potential to participate more intentionally in its expression in the world. The aspects of reality seen from an integrated, awake state of being are not generally apparent or obvious when we are in our usual states of mind, much as the quantum world is not obvious from the perspective of our usual macroworld that obeys Newtonian physics. This does not mean that these aspects of reality are not true. For example, the timeless, relational reality described by quantum physics is always true. It underlies everything we are made of, and is used extensively in modern technology. But it requires special lenses and conditions, different from the ones we most typically use, to be able to see at least the shadow cast by these more hidden aspects of reality. We will get to some of those lenses and conditions later, but first

I want to remind you of the lenses we have (and that we can cultivate) as human beings. Just as rainbows can suddenly appear when the conditions are right, a mystically relational, sparkling reality can spontaneously penetrate our own awareness in moments of clarity.

When is the last time you saw a rainbow? Softly emerging from clouds, at first we may barely make it out—but each time we see those vibrant colors appearing from a gray sky, shining through like a promise, it is amazing all over again. We know that those colors are part of white light all the time, but it is such a gift, such a joyous surprise, each time to see them emerge. So much of what is amazing about our world, our universe, our cosmos, is mostly unapparent to us. Yet in the right conditions we can experience hints of it. Rainbows are revealed when pure sunlight penetrates a field of water droplets diffused through the air, or shines through a prism or crystal.

Similarly, the radio waves of our Bluetooth devices, and all the local radio and television stations that are playing around us, become clear when we have the right receivers to tune them in. And as human beings we also have receivers, faculties we can tune to hear the music of the cosmos. As Sufi mystic Kabir Helminski says:

> We have subtle subconscious faculties that we are not using. Beyond the limited analytic intellect is a vast realm of mind that includes psychic and extrasensory abilities; intuition; wisdom; a sense of unity; aesthetic, qualitative, and creative faculties; and image-forming and symbolic capacities. Though these faculties are many, we give them a single name with some justification, for they are operating best when they are in concert. They comprise an intelligence that is in spontaneous connection with the Universal Intelligence. This total mind we call "heart." [20]

If we limited ourselves to a classical Newtonian paradigm where everything was knowable, separate, and predictable, we might find that anything smacking of spiritual faculties and our own connection to a larger mystery could sound like fantasy. The quantum paradigm, however, involves coherence, tunneling, entanglement, and other phenomena that indicate connections among particles or structures that can't be explained with the classical framework. The interconnected reality tends to be invisible in usual conditions—seeing it also requires specialized scientific tools and specific conditions.

Or, perhaps the deep interconnection described by quantum mechanics could be perceived with an entirely different way of *internal* seeing. This type of mystical seeing is not so rare or impossible: for each of us going about daily life there can be moments when the curtain opens, the light shines through, and we see things as somehow more radiant and alive.

We all have had moments when we suspected greater connections than we noticed—perhaps strolling in a natural setting, seeing a newborn child, or relating deeply to another. And Jesus' words are also full of implications of this oneness, of a mutual indwelling between God and humans, or among humans: "I am in my Father, and you are in me, and I am in you." In his last teachings with his disciples he beautifully says, "I am the vine; you are the branches. Those who abide in me and I in them bear much fruit." He shortly follows this with, "As the Father has loved me, so I have loved you. Abide in my love."[21] What an invitation!

But how do we even begin to access our more subtle faculties in connection with the "heart mind" that Helminski mentions?

How do we access the Wisdom way of knowing?

Wisdom teachers through the centuries have pointed to ways to build our capacity to perceive through a new lens, an integrated Wisdom way of knowing. Insights and openings may happen spontaneously in our lives, but our capacity to attune with them can also be enhanced by daily contemplative practices, including some that look more like meditation, as well as practices that integrate body, mind, and energy such as sacred chanting, yoga and other sacred movements, the arts, and conscious daily work. Coming from more than just the intellect, all of the contemplative practices include a type of self-emptying, or letting go of our usual egoic mind.

Whatever we may say about contemplative practices, it is important to remember that this interconnected, relational reality is not "produced" by anything we might do: we practice "letting go" to it. This is more like consciously joining a stream that is already flowing, or becoming more aware that we are already in it. We are like the proverbial fish swimming in search of water, unaware that it fully surrounds us! According to mystics (and physicists both), this endless stream is constantly bringing forth everything we are made of; the river of life flowing through us exactly as we are, right now. We never produce it or control it; it is at the core of our being. Yet it takes practice to learn to open up to it.

Teachers of Wisdom have classically recommended modalities that can help make us more amenable to the realization of the fullness of the now, such as meditation, Centering Prayer, mindfulness, and Benedictine *ora et labora* (the attempt to establish a daily, intentional rhythm that balances brain, emotions and kinesthetic input—or in other words, three-centered awareness). For most of us westerners, it's a matter of weaning ourselves from our over-dependence on the intellectual center alone; when the others are given space to enter, the rebalancing begins to happen naturally.

Yet what this inter-relational reality actually is will always be a mystery, beyond the reaches of our finite intellect, and beyond anything the equations of physics or words of mystics can precisely convey. Each of these arenas can only point to it, leaving the interpretation and expression of its beauty to our own unique, creative, integrated being, as we consent to our fuller participation in the dance of Wholeness.

Questions for reflection:

- When have you experienced a way of knowing that was not from your intellect?
- What were the qualities of this way of knowing?

Chapter 4

Particles, Waves, and Entanglement
Our Participation in the Cosmic Webs

The common division of the world into subject and object, inner world and outer world, body and soul is no longer adequate.

—Werner Heisenberg

The universe is relational at every level, and even between levels. Relationship is the core and foundational shape of Reality.

—Richard Rohr

Wisdom is an integrated way of knowing that expands our awareness. Science is also expanding our awareness about what we are and our place in the cosmos.

Our physical world, or "cosmic web" can be viewed as a beautiful reflection of Oneness written into the universe by the Source, the Ground of Being, that we are better learning to read. Newton once said that there are two books written by God: the book of scripture, and the book of nature. But when we read the book of nature, it's only when we step back and look on the macroscale of our lives, the scale of our bodies and trees and apples, etc., that the world behaves in more familiar ways. From this point of view, visible to our eyes, Newton's laws of motion can accurately predict the trajectory of an apple falling from a tree, or can be used to plan a flight across time zones or to the moon.

But when we look more closely into the fundamentals of what we are made of, we can get a sense of the wonder that mystics and Wisdom teachers describe. As we zoom in from the macroscale of our everyday world to the quantum scale of molecules and atoms and below, we find a dream-like world where so-called objects (they are more like condensed energy patterns) can pass through energy "walls," and appear and disappear. For example, a tiny electron can pass through a high energy barrier. If the electron were a solid object, it could not achieve enough energy to jump over the barrier, but as a quantum "object" it can tunnel through—the Newtonian physics of solid mechanical objects holds no sway here. Matter on the quantum scale holds far less in terms of absolute form, but far more in terms of possibility and potentiality. Atoms and molecules follow elegant, defined rules, dancing together to the music of wave patterns on a scale tinier than one two-hundred thousandth the thickness of your fingernail. And in some mysterious way, the manner in which we approach reality affects the way it comes back to us—we can begin to see the hidden relationality tucked within it.

Chalice or faces?

What we observe is not nature itself, but nature exposed to our method of questioning.
—**Werner Heisenberg, in** *Physics and Philosophy*

Electrons, atoms, and even molecules aren't rock-like or even water- or sky-like things that we are familiar with. We can touch rocks and water, and breathe air into our lungs. The building blocks of matter are not so simple: they can act both as solid-appearing particles, and also act more non-locally, like waves. These alternate depending on how you look at them. Like the image below in which you might see a chalice or two faces, both are true at the same time. In the case of the image, our eyes usually choose one aspect at a time to see. And once you've seen both, you don't "unsee" them: you can choose which one to bring into awareness.

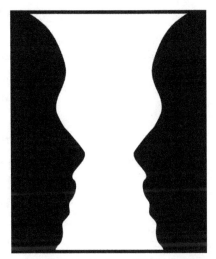

Source: Bryan Derksen, CC BY-SA 3.0
<http://creativecommons.org/licenses/by-sa/3.0/>, via Wikimedia Commons.

Matter exists simultaneously as particles and waves, the latter analogous to a wave on the ocean. But the particle/wave is unlike an ocean wave, which is composed of water molecules, salts, and air that we could hold and see in a container. In quantum mechanics, matter doesn't even actually become matter as we know it *until we observe it*. It's more as though the ocean wave would pass right through me if I weren't looking at it (much as radio waves pass through us all the time without our "noticing").

If this concept of matter as a wave seems baffling, you are not alone—it is a puzzle to scientists as well. To get a better example of how they study this we can have a look at the "slit experiment" to understand how something could possibly be a wave and a particle at the same time, and how our measurements affect it. This experiment might provide better insight into how this mysterious wave behavior points to an inherent relationality, refuting the separateness of things that we usually see on our macroscale.

Waving particles

Can nature possibly be so absurd as it seemed to us in these atomic experiments?
—Werner Heisenberg

At the heart of quantum mechanics is a rule that sometimes governs politicians or CEOs—as long as no one is watching, anything goes.
—Lawrence M. Kraus

Imagine I take a baseball and drop it in a lake. Where I drop it in, it may sink but ripples of waves will spread out. We could say that these waves are sort of like the wave nature of one of our small quantum particles, especially if we propose that the baseball dissolves. Then imagine that the baseball popped right back out of the water, as though one of the waves somehow re-formed itself into the ball. This makes no sense—the wave would have become a solid object.

In a slit experiment a substance (we can call it a particle even though it also behaves like a wave) is launched toward two narrow slits. Scientists have set up the double slit experiment with electrons, atoms, and even large organic molecules composed of numerous atoms, because even these "larger" particles also have a wave nature.[22] This experiment works with light as well. If laser light, for example, is passed through a single slit it will spread evenly. But if it goes through a double slit, the waves emerging from each slit will interact and create an interference[23] pattern of light and dark areas on the detector, just as a wave does.

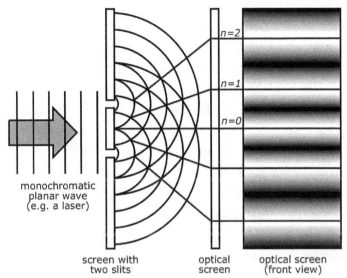

$n=2$

$n=1$

$n=0$

monochromatic
planar wave
(e.g. a laser)

screen with	optical	optical screen
two slits	screen	(front view)

see this interference pattern because waves can add constructively or destructively (they add together, or they cancel to make a dark spot).
Source: Inductiveload, Public domain, via Wikimedia Commons.

The pattern is filled out even when individual photons are sent *one at a time* to the double slit.[24] And the interference pattern is seen also with electrons, atoms, and large organic molecules. Even these "particles" behave like waves: the units that make up all the matter we see are wave-like, interpenetrating and interacting.

The nonduality of the wave/particle

This might seem to make sense, seeing light behave like a wave. But a photon of light behaves as a particle as well. A single photon can kick an electron out of a metal,[25] somewhat like a well-aimed bowling ball can take out a pin. (Digital cameras and other light-sensitive devices take advantage of this.) But even though it acts like a particle, the photon is still a wave as well. We find just one of those forms depending on how we set up the experiment to detect it. Before it is observed, it is fully *both at the same time.* This is one of the aspects of nonduality found within physics.

Another odd behavior in the experiment shows up if we put a detector at each of the double slits. When we do that, the photon will go through *only one* slit or the other, and it does not make an interference pattern. This behavior is because of the Heisenberg uncertainty principle:[26] the more we pin down the photon's position (by placing detectors at the slits to see exactly which slit the photon goes through) the less we know about its momentum, its wave nature.

The way we set up experiments to observe light, electrons, atoms or molecules affects what aspect (wave or particle) we will find. If we set up an experiment that detects the wave nature of an electron (i.e. when we leave position very uncertain—we don't know which slit it travels through) we find more about its momentum, or wave nature; we see it behave like a wave. And if we set up a particle-measuring experiment (where we determine exactly which slit it goes through), particles are what we find. Our very act of measuring selectively chooses what we will see.

We could say that the "particle" before we observe it exists in a non-dual reality. It's not either particle or wave, it's both/*and*. But the lens with which we view it, the way we set up the experiment, colors which aspect of its nondual nature we observe.

What does this mean for us?

> *No phenomenon is a real phenomenon until it is an observed phe-nomenon ... we are participants in bringing into being not only the near and here, but the far away and long ago .*
> **—John Archibald Wheeler**

Our very act of measuring selectively chooses what we will see. This is profound, and has been the subject of much debate about "the observer effect" in scientific circles. It points to the role of the observer, of ourselves, in what we see in the world. We are more like participants who affect the observations than uninvolved watchers. *This is not the same as saying we are creating our own reality.* It is more like saying, reality is highly complex and impossible to grasp all at once.

We are like the blind men and the elephant. Whether each blind man experiences something flat (an ear) or rope-like (a tail) or tree-trunk-like (a leg) depends on which part of the elephant they encounter. In other words, the approach that we use strongly colors what we find. If I look at an elephant through rose-colored glasses, it is going to look pink! But unlike the blind men, we would like to be able to experience the whole elephant. The eyes we need to perceive this may be outside of time (and space) entirely, more like the baffling quantum world.

These puzzling studies point to a relational situation, in a way like the metaphor of viewing the image of the chalice and faces: the lens that we, the experimenter, bring to the world influences the results that we perceive. This participational reality is consistent with the Buddhist concept of interdependent origination, or codependent arising, which asserts that *no object exists independently, but only in relationship with other objects or perceivers.* We can love our neighbor as ourselves because we are not independent of them, or of the world around us. His Holiness the Dalai Lama explains codependent arising as always being in context, for example of our shared language, social conventions, and also shared fundamental accepted knowledge base, all of which vary among different cultures.[27] He says: "What is meant by emptiness ...? It is not the emptiness of existence but rather the emptiness of true or independent existence, which means that things exist by dependence upon other factors."[28]

The concept of an observer effect evokes for me an implication that we can become more active participants in this interrelated reality, this mysterious web of being, than we usually realize. In *Always a Pilgrim*, Father Thomas Hand, a Catholic priest who brought Eastern meditation to Mercy Center in Burlingame, California, said: "Where attention goes, energy flows, and life grows." In other words, the way we meet the world affects the way in which it meets us. If I'm having a crabby morning, I will likely find lots of opportunities to engage with things that will increase that crabbiness, or provide me with an opportunity to wrestle with someone or something. On a morning when I am at peace, the world seems more peaceful. The overall events may be the same: I am not saying that we are actually changing events; this is more subtle. But the way we approach the world affects the way we experience it.

Talking about the effect of our own energy on the world, Cynthia Bourgeault wrote:

> This refers to the subtler energies, which science does not at this point measure but which we know have a real impact on our physical world. These would include the energies of attention, will, prayer, and love. Although no mathematical equation presently exists that can describe the force of attention, it is simple enough in real life to observe the difference in effectiveness between a job done with attention and a job done without it. And while there is no formula governing how love makes things grow, we have only to look at a child who is neglected to see that some vital ingredient is in fact conveyed through the act of loving. There are no theorems or formalisms to describe it, but an energetic transaction is clearly taking place.[29]

She describes an energetic transaction: we, as observers and participants, can affect the world around us by our attention and intention. More poetically speaking, the way we meet the universe affects the way it is reflected back to us.

Looking at matter: a perspective beyond spacetime

The illusion of space and time that continues around us is a blurred vision of the swarming of elementary processes, just as a calm, clear Alpine lake consists in reality of a rapid dance of myriads of minuscule water molecules.
—**Carlo Rovelli, in** *Seven Brief Lessons on Physics*

Let's look into what scientists say about the slit experiment, a particular type of interaction with a quantum object. Physicist John Wheeler, as well as some philosophers, have said that the observer "creates" a reality by the choices made, e.g. by setting up the experiment in a particular way that will measure either a particle or a wave. In this experiment, scientific instruments cannot directly detect the nondual reality in which an atom, electron, or photon is both wave and particle at the same time, but the way we choose to measure it affects what aspects of this greater reality we will see.

Physicist Richard Feynman's explanation of the quantum phenomena in the slit experiment blew a lot of minds. He proposed a wild-sounding mathematical formulation for the wave/particle phenomenon that would produce the wave interference pattern, but without bringing waves into it at all. He proposed that quantum objects such as electrons are not "things" limited to our 4D spacetime (three spatial dimensions plus time) at all, and hence the particle can travel multiple paths at once.[30] Christophe Galfard described a particle following Feynman's formulation: "Quantum particles do not behave like tennis balls, but like the quantum particles they are. To get from one place to another, they take all the possible paths in space and time as long as these paths link their starting point to their end point. The particle ... literally went everywhere. Simultaneously. To the left and to the right of the post. And through it. And outside the room. And into the future and back—until the moment when it hit a detector on the wall."[31]

Feynman's proposal seems rather impossible, unless we consider that time and space are far more complex and multidimensional than we usually think. We can't fully know or understand the nature of the fundamental particles that make up our world using our usual emphasis on 4D spacetime. When we set up an experiment to observe them, we see only one aspect of them: for example, only particle or only wave behavior in the slit experiment, but not the full wave/particle nature all at once. It as though we are seeing only a minor aspect of a field of higher dimensionality as it dips into our 4D spacetime reality. It's quite a puzzle! Hence, Feynman's quote: "it is my task to convince you *not* to turn away because you don't understand it. You see, my physics students don't understand it either. That is because *I* don't understand it. Nobody does."[32]

Thinking in this way can be disorienting, because we don't usually perceive the world this way. But just as Feynman accepts that we can't and won't really understand it, we are not expecting to, either. But I encourage you to notice how perhaps your ways of thinking about things might be being stretched, or opened a bit as we explore these topics. The suspension of our need to grasp with just our minds is key to sinking into the mystery of our relational reality.

Feynman's explanation that a quantum particle can take all possible paths to get to the detector is not the only interpretation for the wave/particle conundrum. Let's look at how some other scientists have approached the mystery of the nondual quantum world revealed in the slit experiment. For instance, some envision unobserved particles as being in many states at the same time. Quantum entanglement and quantum teleportation, which are used in quantum computing,[33] can also be explained in terms of these many states. Matter is far more complex than we usually acknowledge it to be, and possibly exists outside of 4D spacetime entirely!

Superposition: Many things at the same time

The wave-and-particle-like representation (we'll call it "Psi," for short) of a particle before it is observed has been shown to be many things at once. This is called a "superposition," or the simultaneous existence of several states, with different energies and shapes at the same time. (Maybe it sounds supernatural!) This simultaneous existence of a particle in many conditions at the same time may be confusing perhaps to think about, but let's continue with it, because superposition underlies a lot of the phenomena we see in quantum mechanics.

We are familiar with states of matter, e.g. water in liquid, solid (ice) and gas (steam) states. In a superposition all would exist at the same time—not as a mixture of all three where some are ice, some liquid and some vapor[34]—but for each group of water molecules to somehow be

28

all three at the same time. That's as difficult to visualize as a single insect being an egg, caterpillar, and butterfly all at the same time!

But being multiple things at the same time is not inconsistent with Feynman's theory: if the particle exists outside of time it *could* be many things at once; just as a butterfly might be viewed as an egg, caterpillar, chrysalis, and butterfly if viewed outside of time. When we observe a particle, for example with the detector in the slit experiment, we see only a single one of those states. This is sometimes called "collapsing" Psi, meaning we're seeing one of the many possibilities in its array of many.

A "black box" approach

In the widely used Copenhagen interpretation of quantum physics, we accept that the little slice of electron life we find smashed onto our detector tells us the entire story, or at least all we need to know. This theory says that Psi, which is many states at once, collapses to just one state when we observe it. We dismiss the rest as though they don't exist anymore because, in our 4D spacetime, we are generally capable of observing only one state at a time. We can't easily capture the multiple states so we choose not to think about them. (Although this feat of capturing multiple states can be accomplished in particular conditions.)[35]

In the double slit experiment, we detect any single particle in just one place, sometimes called a "collapse" of all its superpositions. In the Copenhagen interpretation, the observer's knowledge of the wave/particle collapses to one state when it is detected, i.e. when a particle collides with the macroscopic world (such as when a particle hits a camera or detector screen), however there is no conjecture about what Psi might be, or what the nature of the particle/wave is before it is observed. One pragmatic form of the Copenhagen interpretation could be stated simply: we don't know what Psi really means; let's just apply it because it works. Scientists do this all the time, using quantum mechanics to calculate properties and develop aspects of our current technologies, without focusing a whole lot on what Psi means.

We do know that a quantum object is much less like solid matter, and more like possibility. Psi is sometimes called a "probability wave" because its shape lays out the area where the particle is most likely to be found when we observe or detect it.[36] Such lack of definiteness about location and state is non-intuitive for us, but we are not alone in that—it led Einstein to grumpily state about quantum mechanics, "God does not play dice with the universe."

As a probability wave, Psi has a larger amplitude where the particle is more likely to be found, and a smaller amplitude where it is less likely. For example, if your location over the course of this day were a wave function (a mathematical way of describing the multiple states in Psi) it might have a significant amplitude at your local coffee shop, or other favorite hangout. It might have an even higher amplitude around your house, your place of work, and perhaps in your neighborhood where you took a walk this morning. If you had a piece of permanent chalk drawing on the ground wherever you went over time, the intensity of the chalk at one of those places and other favorite frequents would be significant, but less so at places you've only been to once. But because we are not quantum particles we are in only one of these places at a time (at least that is our usual perception of it!). Psi can be in many states, with different energies and configurations, at the same time before we measure it. (Or, it exists outside of time as Feynman proposed.) And yet in other interpretations of quantum mechanics, there are implications that we are far more connected than we usually realize, much as the mystics tell us.

Many worlds: One single wave function

In another interpretation that Hugh Everett (in 1957) called "austere quantum mechanics," Psi doesn't collapse at all. We don't lose all those other aspects of the superposition that existed before measurement: our little quantum particle gets resurrected from its lifeless blip on the detector wall. Instead, this interpretation says there is one continuous wave function that evolves smoothly. But there is another mind-blowing cost: the process of measurement, for example in the slit experiment, can be thought to create many worlds, each with one of the possible results for the experiment. Hence austere quantum mechanics is sometimes called the "many worlds" theory.[37] According to this formulation, the electrons, detector, observer, and even the whole universe are part of *one single wave function*. The superposition of the electron before measurement evolves into a superposition of different worlds. In each of these worlds the observer has detected the electron in just one of its states. If you were the experimenter, you wouldn't be aware of all these worlds.

If you find yourself uncomfortable imagining many worlds, you are in good company! The main point is that our cosmos is far more multifaceted than our usual notions of 4D spacetime, and more connected than we usually perceive it to be. The Wisdom traditions also identify multiple realms. For example, Cynthia Bourgeault lays out Gurdjieff's many worlds, each with different densities, in *Eye of the Heart*.[38] Tibetan Buddhism identifies six different realms, including the human and animal realms, and Jesus also refers to many other abodes ("In my Father's house there are many dwelling places," John 14:2, NRSV).

However, rather than insisting on many worlds, physicist Sean Carroll describes austere quantum mechanics in a different way: "The truth is, nothing forces us to think of the wave function as describing multiple worlds.... We could just talk about the entire wave function as a whole. It's just really helpful to split it up into worlds."[39] Austere quantum mechanics points to one unified wave function, one Wholeness that includes everything, and is not at all subject to the typical patterns we observe for spacetime. With ordinary tools such as the detectors used in the slit experiment, we only see a partial picture of this unified wave function, our "collapsed" electron, and it can be difficult to extrapolate back to the wild freedom of the electron before measurement, or the "whole elephant."

There are so many wonders tucked into the core of what we are, and what we are made of. As Jesus said in the Gospel of Thomas, a text found at Nag Hammadi in 1945, "What your own eyes cannot see, your human ears do not hear, your physical hands cannot touch, and what is inconceivable to the human mind—that I will give to you!"[40] Whatever those wonders are that Jesus was talking about, we know that we grasp only a partial picture of our amazing reality with our usual faculties. Looking with the eyes of science can help us to see, to step back, and see more of the whole, and perhaps inspire the mystic within us to wake up and see as well.

Let's look at more implications of superposition, this phenomenon of being many things at once or outside of 4D spacetime entirely. It underlies some other phenomena "inconceivable to the human mind" as well, pointing to the cosmic, interconnected, interwoven web we are talking about.

Schrödinger's infamous hypothetical cat, being in a superposition of both alive and dead, would somehow be in both states at the same time.
Source: https://www.clipartmax.com/middle/
m2i8A0K9b1H7Z5K9_schr%C3%B6dingers-cat-illustration-sherodinger-cat/.

Wanted: Schrödinger's cat, dead *and* alive

You may have heard of Schrödinger's poor hypothetical cat. In this thought experiment, devised by Schrödinger to look at the absurdity of the Copenhagen interpretation, a cat is left in a box with a cylinder of poisonous gas, and a radioactive atom that has a 50-50 chance of decaying. If the atom leaves its 50-50 (decayed/not decayed) quantum superposition and decays, it hits a Geiger counter that triggers open the valve to the poisonous gas and immediately kills the cat. If it doesn't decay, the cat stays alive. Until we open the box, we have no idea whether the atom has decayed, and according to the Copenhagen interpretation as long as the box is kept closed the cat is said to be in a superposition of these two states, both 50% alive and 50% dead *at the same time.* (As Monday mornings sometimes feel.) Only when the box is opened would we find a single one of these states, an alive or dead cat. In other words, when we actually observe it the cat's nondual, both-alive-and-dead nature, would collapse to just one of those possibilities: a single state, like our electron smashed on the detector wall.[41]

The law of three

We love to think in terms of either/or, alive/dead, or particle/wave. We want to *know* which it is and have it decided; put into a box with no need to ponder any further. However, Wisdom teachings arise entirely outside of dualistic, or even time-bound thinking. The law of three, for example, sees a ternary principle operating in many situations: this consists of first force (affirming), second force (denying), and third force (reconciling, or neutralizing). The action of third force results in an entirely new arising. Thus, the law of three can be far more dynamic and creative than a simple binary system.

For example, in photosynthesis, which I studied in my PhD program, in the plant system that makes molecular oxygen, water interacts with an enzyme (called the water oxidation complex). But it is light, the third force, that brings the complex through several steps to a new arising: molecular oxygen! In a simpler system, there is a bell in my garden. It is lifted by the rope attaching it to the eaves, and the clapper hangs down. When a strong enough wind (a third force) blows through the yard, the bell rings and makes a sound, a new arising. I imagine the arising of music through many different instruments can involve this type of interaction. And then the music can act as a new force, resulting for example in dancing and a joyous atmosphere.

Humans, too, are thought to have a mysterious role at the intersection of the horizontal, with all the time-bound activity of daily life and this world, and the vertical, our relationship with the spiritual, with what lies beyond time. It is said that we have a role to play in this unique position; the potential to invite third force and participate in the creation of a new arising. I think we do this all the time in our interactions with each other and the world, offering fruits of the spirit such as kindness, gentleness, peacefulness, etc. even in the midst of conflicts where two opposing forces seem at a stand-off. I'll continue to unwrap this in the following chapters, but for now I'd like to return to science and its evidence of superposition, in real-world Schrödinger's cat type experiments.

Alive and dead at the same time

The hypothetical Schrödinger's cat experiment may sound bizarre, but actual experiments (on a scale much smaller than a cat) have confirmed superpositions of particles being in at least two states at once. These experiments become more difficult as the number of particles involved increases, but scientists keep performing them with larger and larger assemblies of particles. They will likely never involve something as complex as a cat, but they are still called "cat" states, in honor of Schrödinger's mythical friend.[42]

In one Schrödinger's-cat-type experiment, a pile of atoms defied our 4D spacetime. Scientists were able to find the same cluster of atoms (10,000 rubidium atoms) in *two places at once*, separated by more than half a meter (about 21 inches apart).[43] (Imagine the possibilities if we humans could pull that one off?!) Scientists are also working on "cat" states involving multiple atoms relevant for quantum computing.[44] They can even have some control of this quantum information and save Schrödinger's poor cat by predicting quantum jumps, previously thought to be far more random, before they happen.[45] Rather than letting it collapse into the equivalent of a live or dead cat, they can bring it back into its quantum superposition of being both at the same time. It lives!

Entanglement, or "Spooky action at a distance"

The strange phenomenon of superposition results in other odd, non-intuitive behaviors, in which particles can behave as though they are connected even though they may be very far apart. Because of quantum superpositions (and also via quantum fields, as we will soon see) we can get a phenomenon called entanglement. Imagine that I have two quantum cats, under each of two magician's hats. I know for sure that when I look, I will find one cat alive and the other one dead, but there is no way to determine which is which. In their spooky quantum superposition, each cat is equally likely alive and dead at the same time. If I lift one hat to reveal a cat that is alive and scampering off to get away from me, the other cat is instantaneously forced out of its superposition and declared dead, *even if the other hat was on the other side of the planet*, or even the other side of the universe. As soon as its entangled partner is coaxed into our four-dimensional spacetime by our measurement, it too is dragged along. Splat!

Because the two cats in hats were entangled, when I collapse Psi for one of them, the other no longer has a 50-50 chance of being in either state: it instantaneously collapses to the other state of the superposition. It's not a matter of information traveling from one particle to the other—they have proven that it happens much more quickly than possible for this, no matter how far away. Both are initially part of the same "super-thing," and remain so.

This is called quantum entanglement. (Birds are thought to navigate by quantum entanglement of molecules in their retina, for example, using this to sense the earth's magnetic field.)[46] Quantum entanglement has also been called "spooky action at a distance," by Einstein, who didn't believe that it could possibly be true. But, unlimited by the speed of light (the so-called "speed limit" for the universe), a measurement of one entangled particle can *instantaneously* force the state of the other, no matter how far away it is. And particles that start out in a quantum superposition can remain correlated, or entangled, no matter how far apart they may be.

Entangled photons on mountains in Tibet

This might sound a bit fanciful, but entanglement has been measured in scientific experiments. For example, entangled photons were measured 1200 km apart when a satellite named Micius beamed the photons down to two mountains in Tibet.[47] High mountains were chosen in order to minimize interference from earth's atmosphere. The photons were "correlated," or shown to be intimately connected in entanglement, significantly more than would be seen by chance alone. Scientists have also managed to entangle millions of atoms in a centimeter-sized crystal[48] and entangle rubidium atoms over dozens of kilometers through coiled optical fiber.[49] And you thought *your* toys were fun!

Teleportation: Beam me up, Scotty.

Entanglement also has possibilities for quantum teleportation. This is not quite as sexy as it sounds—it's not like the transporters that "beam" people from one place to another in *Star Trek*; it's more like a quick-change act: a quantum state can be sent to another particle, replacing the original state of the receiving particle. For example, information can be passed between two computer chips without any wired connection, using only quantum teleportation.[50] This may have practical uses: quantum teleportation has the potential for super-encryption of data that could avoid interception by hackers. Scientists have achieved quantum teleportation using microwaves, relevant for quantum computing,[51] and through a 10.8-foot-long tank of sea water[52] and up to a satellite 1400 km away.[53]

In summary, the building blocks of everything we see are far less tangible or defined than we usually think. There is nothing really there, in the sense of hard matter, yet there is more, in the sense of possibility. Particles can exist in many states at the same time, and in more than one place at the same time. We can measure their connection via entanglement or teleportation across long distances. And there is a mysterious connection between observer and observed, in that choices in measurement bring just one possibility of the superposition into evidence. (Or perhaps many worlds, each with just one of those possibilities.) This points to an intimate, relational engagement of our macroscopic world, seemingly rooted in 4D spacetime, with the mysterious unfolding web of reality.

Questions for reflection:

- How are your ways of thinking about the world being stretched, or opened a bit as we explore these topics?
- Consider your relationships with people who have a different view from you, politically or personally. What happens when you aim to see things from their point of view as well as your own: if you come in seeking to understand, how is that different from when you come in intending to convince someone that you are right and they are wrong?
- In what situations in your life have you felt third force come in—something unexpected, and beyond any impasse you might have felt?
- Many of the concepts here may be difficult to grasp, because they don't follow our usual perception of reality as seen in our macroworld. It may be helpful to view them more as Zen koans, or parables: these make no sense from the ordinary mind. Suspension of the need to grasp with just the mind is key to sinking in to the mystery of our relational reality. How does it feel, to take your sense of the need to know and relax it a bit. Is it scary? Mind-opening? Or both?

Chapter 5

Coherence and Wholeness

A good gauge of spiritual health is to write down the three things
you most want. If they in any way differ, you are in trouble.

—Rumi[54]

What is essential vs. what is merely interesting

Coherence is an important factor in quantum physics, and also in Wisdom studies. We'll talk about both, but start off with its implications in Wisdom work. The term "coherence" is sometimes used in Wisdom circles to talk about a way of being in which our intentions and actions are aligned. In the Gurdjieff work people talk about "A" influences and "B" influences. Some typical A influences include trendy items such as what's new on social media, what brands or styles of clothing are in and out, or what's the latest cool vegetable that everyone is growing or preparing. This also extends to spiritual circles, as in, *This year this guru is hot, let's drop all the old stuff and go see them.* Or being distracted from an important event such as, *I was going to go to this retreat with a teacher I really resonate with, but it overlaps with my cousin's birthday party.* These impulses pull you in one direction and another, and are somewhat analogous to waves out of phase: they cancel each other out. In discussing A and B influences, Cynthia Bourgeault often tells a story that Alan Jones, Dean Emeritus of Grace Cathedral in San Francisco, told on himself. He had a spiritual director who said, "Alan, you must learn to tell the difference between what's essential and what's merely interesting."

Jesus told several parables about these influences. For example: "Again, the kingdom of heaven is like a merchant looking for fine pearls. When he found one of great value, he went away and sold everything he had and bought it" (Matthew 13:45-46, NIV). This sounds like Jesus, a Wisdom teacher, is talking about a B influence (the pearl of great value) that is worth more than everything else the merchant had (A influences). Once you find the pearls of great value, the most meaningful influences in your life, you are encouraged to let go of the craving for the small ones. You learn to see that the small ones waste your time and basically get you nowhere.

Gradually, as we do our spiritual work and learn to have coherence in our being, we learn to distinguish what might be merely a surface influence from one that has deeper meaning and implications, or a B influence. These feel different: B influences have a deeper resonance with who we really are, and where our deeper being is drawn to move, grow, and flourish. B influences are not based on appearance, trendiness, or even what we think we are supposed to be doing.

The pearl is within you

You may learn to notice a quiet voice inside that gently urges you in a particular direction. It may not seem flashy, special, or even very noticeable in the midst of a busy life. Hearing it is enhanced by practices that quiet down the insides, like the classic spiritual metaphor of letting the mud settle in a pool so that you can see clearly. Rather than constantly looking outside ourselves to the newest, shiniest thing that we think is going to help us get enlightened, we instead learn to attune within. There is a Quaker saying: "Keep within. And when they say, 'Look here or look there is Christ,' go not forth, for Christ is within you. And those who try to draw your minds away from the teaching inside you, are opposed to Christ. For the measure's within, and the light of God is within, and the pearl is within you, though hidden."[55]

A meditation practice will help you do this. Not because it will bring you great peace or insights, but because it shows you how to stay steady, to hold the course, whatever influences come into your mind, emotions, or sensations as you sit. You grow a new inner compass that is not dependent on outer influences. When you learn to stay steady in your practice and notice the difference in your life between A and B influences, to recognize the pearl of great value, then a teacher of "C" influence can come into your life.

"C" Influences

Really good spiritual teachers are hard to find. You're not likely to find them via a flashy web site and huge, popular events. They may not wear robes or fancy headdresses (unless they legitimately come from a culture where that is done). But when you consistently learn to distinguish what is merely interesting from what is truly important, then a C-influence teacher can come along. Because before that there is really nothing they could show you—you wouldn't know the value of it. And being with them can be tough. Steven Tainer, my first Wisdom teacher, likened being near the teacher as being next to a refiner's fire. They are not going to cater to your ego, to your sense of identification and importance. They will peel you open, and crack open the shell that covers the pith of the seed that is you; the seed that can transform and grow to a tree and produce fruit.

When you are alert to B influences, you learn not to waste your time with pursuits that will take you in circles but instead to gather in your energy, your intention. You look within, to the pearl of great value, and your being acts as one coherent whole.

About coherence

The term "coherence" is also used in science. One characteristic is that a system acts together as a single whole. This can result in odd behavior such as a pile of atoms appearing in two places at the same time, fluid that can run uphill, or superconductors that can lift an entire train. Some limitations to achieving quantum coherence in macroscopic objects (like humans, and cats) are that we are made up of a huge number particles—the many different parts of us are doing very different things. So, even though everything in our experience is made up of particles that are subject to quantum rules, we don't usually experience odd quantum effects with objects around us. We don't generally put our hands through walls like electrons that tunnel though high barriers, and we can't go through two separate doors at the same time like quantum particles in the slit experiment. Coherence is being studied on the relatively large nanoscale,[56] but even biological organisms can demonstrate quantum properties.

Entanglement and coherence in quantum biology

The field of quantum biology looks at processes in biological systems that involve quantum phenomena such as coherence, tunneling, and entanglement. Biological organisms have a lot of processes going on, often in warm, moist environments. We wouldn't call them overall coherent systems, but they too are capable of quantum effects. For example, quantum tunneling occurs in proton transfer reactions in DNA and enzymes. In photosynthetic systems coherent energy transfer can be far more efficient than in a classical model because the transfer takes multiple paths simultaneously—and the most efficient one predominates! Likewise, avian magnetoreception (bird navigation) is thought to involve entanglement.[57]

Coherent states in physics

In the experiments we talked about where piles of atoms appeared in two places at once, the atoms were very cold so that the wave patterns were coherent, becoming more like *one whole thing* instead of separate parts. When helium is in a coherent state, for example, a phenomenon that happens when it gets nearly as cold as the outer universe (−455 degrees Fahrenheit, or -270 degrees Celcius), it starts to show bizarre behavior and can flow uphill and out of a container, in frictionless movement. It's then called a superfluid.

Superconductors enter a state of coherence also, called super-conductivity,[58] where the electrons in a solid all enter a single state. (Electrons are a type of particle called fermions, and they don't usually like to do that.) The electron composite then acts as a single connected fluid and their coherence can lift an entire train! Maglev trains can travel at nearly 600 kilometers per hour (360 mph) because they don't actually touch the track—they perform a levitating trick above it. Floating hoverboards[59] use this trick too.

Quantum "clicks" in mind and matter

"Two stones cannot occupy the same space at the same time. But two fra-grances can," writes the Sufi philosopher Kabir Helminski. Matter undergoes a transition from a substance somewhat like stones, to something more like a fragrance: there is a sudden "click" into a new configuration when helium is cooled to the right temperature to make a superfluid, or when a substance becomes superconductive. In this new state, properties change so radically that it is sometimes called a new phase of matter (remember that other common phases are solids, liquids and gases). But, in fact, it changes from one entire category of matter to another. It starts as fermions, which like to stay separate. This is why matter feels solid even though it's mostly empty space; it's because electrons and other particles are fermions that are more stone-like. There is a sudden transition to another category (called bosons) that behave more like a fragrance, where two or more can mix in the same state.[60] Light is a type of boson. Unlike fermions, many bosons, such as light particles, can be in the same state at the same time: that's how we get powerful lasers.

Quantum clicks during meditation

This type of quantum click sounds a bit like a transformation described by meditators. During contemplative practice, many people describe a spontaneous transition to a more open state, with a feeling of connection and timelessness. And when a group of people meditate together, many have described a "click" to a sense of resonance that includes all in the room. I have felt this on Centering Prayer retreats, usually a couple of days in. It begins to feel as though there is only one meditator in the room, or that some mysterious cloud of energy includes all of us; we are connected as one whole.

In a deep, contemplative state, which we have previously called Wisdom mind, primordial presence, or "seeing with the heart," meditators have noticed less of a sense of separation, or being caught up in a linear time-driven mode, and more openness to a timeless possibility. We could poetically say that a group of people in contemplative practice can become more like the "composite electrons" in a superconductor that suddenly act as bosons. They become more like a fragrance, less bound by rules of separation. A type of "quantum click" to coherence in the brain has actually been measured in contemplative monks. We will see that data later.

What does it mean for us?

We are invited to entertain the possibility of our own entanglement—with each other, and with more than we can imagine, in an intimate interwoven connection beyond 4D spacetime. And as we will discuss, prayer, or the deep intention to hold up the wellbeing of another, can be immensely powerful, as part of this Wisdom way of interbeing. We are far more intimately connected than we usually realize, and when we act coherently, with our intention aligned with qualities such as the fruits of the spirit (e.g. generosity, patience, gentleness), we affect the entire cosmos. Remember, coherence can lift an entire train!

Questions for reflection:

- Name a few A influences in your life that tend to entrain you in a busy cycle without much time to pay attention to things that are more important.

- What are the most important B influences in your life? What helps you to listen to them, to cultivate them? How does it feel when you respond to them?
- As you ponder the concepts of coherence and entanglement, how do you imagine these concepts might apply to you, and your own experiences?

Chapter 6

Nothing is Independent of Anything Else
The Dance of Exchange

Giving-is-receiving is the energetic frequency upon which our universe is aligned. All other approaches to energy exchange immediately cause dissonance and disharmony in our life experience.
—**Michael Brown, in** *The Presence Process*

We have seen that physics points to a cosmos that is highly relational. Particles can remain in intimate relationship across long distances, and measurement of one affects its intimate partner instantaneously, no matter how far away. In a richly interpenetrative reality, there is a constant dance of exchange. And we experience a vibrant exchange—in our bodies, with other beings, with our environment, and with the whole universe.

We are made of stardust

Take a moment to sense your own body breathing. As you breathe in air, and exchange the oxygen we take in for the carbon dioxide we breathe out, notice how your body moves as part of that dance of exchange—perhaps your belly or chest is rising and falling in rhythm. Your eyes are responding to light as you read this, with an exchange of chemistry and brain signals. Your ears may be responding to sounds. Your skin sensitively responds to air passing over it or to temperature changes, or to the gentle pressure of your hand or foot resting on a surface. Our bodies are deeply connected with the world around us.

A dynamic exchange is inherent in all biology, within and among organisms and their environment. Trees exchange nutrients and information via the microorganisms living within their root systems. Water is exchanged along streams and ecosystems, is evaporated and condensed into clouds, and returns to streams etc. as rain. We exchange air in our lungs, nutrients in our digestive and circulatory systems, we drink and excrete water through our pores and elimination systems, and we eat food and let go of what we don't need to keep. All of these open systems, where there is a constant exchange with the outside world and other beings, remind us that we are intimately related with our environment in a dynamic exchange.

In physics, there is a dynamic exchange between energy and mass, as particles collide and create new particles, or in nuclear reactions where large amounts of energy are released from mass. And there is exchange in chemistry: even a system at equilibrium is still in a dynamic state of exchange between reactants and products.

We exchange energy: our power needs may be supplied to us from a broad infrastructure. We receive energy from our sun, a source of warmth and of all our food as it nourishes plants and other photosynthetic organisms. Likewise, we exchange with our planet: we walk on the earth, breathe the air it holds close, reap its fruits, and hopefully tend to its health as best we can, sometimes just by deeply appreciating its gifts. And we are personally related to the stars—we are made from stardust, from explosions of stars that created the elements found in our bodies.

We are intimately connected: none of us is independent of anyone else, or of the cosmos around us. Exchange can be magical among people—wherever people are, we are drawn to find a way to connect, to help one another. A simple smile to or from our neighbor on the grocery line changes the energy around and between us, bringing at least a moment of joy and a sense of abundance. We have an inner compass that knows what feels right, in whatever circumstances we find ourselves. Our giving and receiving nurture us, confirming our connection with the highly interrelated cosmos. I'm reminded again of the Buddhist concept of interdependent arising: our experience is intimately interwoven with other beings, and with the conditions that surround us.

The exchange occurs on more subtle levels as well. We can sometimes sense when someone enters the room, or is looking at us, even when we can't see them. As someone approaches us, we can sense benevolent or hostile energy. Of course, some of this is body language, but our bodies also generate fields: EEG and EKG measurements are used to probe just two of these biofields. With sensitive instruments the field generated by the human heart can be measured out to distances several feet away from the body.

Mercy: Jesus points to a dynamic exchange

I am the vine; you are the branches. If you remain in me and I in you, you will bear much fruit; apart from me you can do nothing.
—John 15:5

The concept of exchange rings throughout Jesus' teachings, as well. In the Beatitudes Jesus tells us, "Blessed are the merciful, for they will receive mercy" (Matthew 5:7, NRSV). In Aramaic, the language Jesus spoke, there is not a specific future tense, but tenses for actions that are completed and those that are not completed. So, this could also mean, "Blessed are the merciful for they are obtaining mercy." In other words, this Beatitude may not indicate a cause and effect, but an *instantaneous reciprocity*: as we are merciful, we are also receiving mercy. The word mercy itself, if you look at the Latin, comes from the same root as merchant, or mercantile, implying a transaction. This discussion of exchange, mercy, echoes for me of the exchange intimated in Shakespeare's *Merchant of Venice*: "The quality of mercy is not strain'd. It droppeth as the gentle rain from heaven upon the place beneath. It is twice blest: It blesseth him that gives and him that takes."

When we look further back at the Semitic roots of the word usually translated as "mercy" in the Beatitudes, we see that it arises from the tri-consonant root r-h-m (we could write it as *rachem* or *rachma*), a verb translated as "to love, or to be merciful or compassionate."[61] Its Semitic etymology also denotes a womb, or uterus. Thus, this quality of mercy, also translated as compassion, denotes a nurturing that is not earned but bestowed. It is an invitation to love one another the way a mother loves her children: with kindness and calming compassion. The intimate inter-abiding of the womb is also echoed in "I am the vine, you are the branches," and "On that day you will know that I am in my father, and you in me, and I in you" (John 14:20, NRSV). This emphasizes the dynamic, interwoven exchange between humans and Jesus, Jesus and God, and thus humans and God. Yet this mercy, this divine exchange, is not something you can create; it is more like an en-wombing field you let go to or sink into.

Mercy is also something we can offer to one another, and to the cosmos. What would the world be like if we offered a nurturing, accepting, and embracing space for others in the world, whatever their differences from us—ethnicity, background, political, or religious preferences? That doesn't mean we need to accept everything a person has done—we may even need to distance ourselves from them—but rather to hold them in our hearts acknowledging the loving, interwoven and interabiding Oneness that pulses through everything. In our hyper-connected universe, we share one field, one large entangled cosmos beyond time and space. To me, it begins to sound a lot like "Love your neighbor as yourself"—not with pity or in spite of difference, but because we are more intimately related than we could usually begin to imagine.

Oneness on the road

One day a curtain opened and I had the shock of seeing this intimate relatedness clearly. I had just completed a walking pilgrimage into Rome with my husband Paul. As we sat down, exhausted, the next day in the Pantheon, my heart was thrown wide open. A young woman sat down in the row ahead of me, her long dark hair held back in a scarf. I couldn't see her whole face, but as I looked I was struck with a sense of recognition and joy—she *was* me, *is* me, somehow. I knew this didn't really make sense, but somehow it was also true. I could sense her life with intimacy, as though it were mine too and mine were hers. The moment felt radiant and full of a super-aliveness, with more dimension and sense of reality than I've usually experienced. It was unencumbered by any previous thoughts, ideas, or histories. I loved her! After looking at her for a while, puzzled at how she could seem so much inside of me, so beloved, even though we'd never met, I gazed around in bewildered amazement. I took in all the people circulating the room, their many whispers creating a gentle buzz. I looked a few rows ahead and my eyes rested on another woman, maybe forty-ish, with dark curly hair an inch or two long and a soft, gentle face. Again, I felt a recognition and almost a sense of being inside her life—she *is* me! And the man with her—my mind wrestled with this as though it couldn't possibly be—but he too was me. I had trouble imagining myself in his life, a man and so different from me, but knew it was somehow true. It felt like the whole room had been opened up, turned inside out, another dimension revealed laughing out loud as the truth that had been there the whole time.

This curtain was open only for a few minutes, but I wonder about the circumstances that helped me to see it better. I had just walked into Rome from nearly 200 km further north, along an old pilgrimage route, the Via Francigena.[62] The pilgrimage was not my idea. My husband Paul is drawn to these long-distance prayer treks, intuiting that they are what he needs to thrive, to more fully inhabit his life in this crazy, busy world. He had begun walking this particular trip in Switzerland and I happily joined him for the last bit of it, imagining a romantic trek through the hills of Tuscany and Lazio with enough healthy exercise to earn all the pasta and wine we would enjoy. But the trip was hard.

Each fall day would start with the fresh dew of joy and hope, walking through green hills framed by cyprus trees, olives, and groves of ripe hazelnuts. Filling my lungs with crisp morning air, I took in the birdsong, almost as if I could almost understand it, a language I somehow used to know. Paul called this starry-eyed beginning of the day's walk "stage one," before fatigue sets in. Urgently aware of the unusual beauty of the morning, I sometimes felt a wave of sadness—I wanted to capture it, take it home with me. I'd remind myself, *be here*, take in the beauty—and then I would welcome it into my belly as fully part of me, instead of wanting to compact it and slip it into a backpack full of memories.

Yet my feet would rush forward, knowing we had far to go, wanting to GET THERE before the day went on too long. But after about ten-ish miles—entering stage two, according to Paul—the blisters on my feet began to raise their complaints despite specialized bandages, gel inserts, and attempts to tie my shoes differently. I worked to convince myself I wasn't really walking barefoot on metal spikes and doomed to pain for eternity. With many miles to go, there was no way through but forward. No Uber to call, no taxi to hail, no bus route through these anachronistic hill towns and the space between them. It was one tenderly placed step after the other, up the steep road to the next hill, down and up again to the next.

Joy and Paul on the Via Francigena in Italy, on the path between Vetralla and Capranica.

There was no way I could make this journey with my usual monkey-mind jumping around—wondering why I had gotten myself into this, or why Paul was crazy enough to love this stuff, or simmering in resentment at my poor feet or at the raw heat on my back. This long journey couldn't work like that. So I kept letting go. Resting my eyes on a spot up the road, I could take in just the next thirty feet or so of the journey at a time, instead of worrying about the multiple kilometers ahead. As my eyes flitted to the next respite, be it a rock or a bush, it felt as though the road ahead was part of me: anchored in my body, it seemed to reel me into itself by an invisible thread. I went into what sometimes felt like a trance: no thoughts, just my body and the road: letting go over and over, letting the trail draw me in, leading me from something greater than my own myopic sense of limitation. As we walked, sometimes a Taizé[63] song chanted in the background of my awareness. Or a pleading rose from my heart: to accept and be present with this, with my body just as it was, in the midst of whatever was coming up. This was somewhat like the meditation practice I do, Centering Prayer, but the out-on-the-road version. The let-go-and-let-God-because-on-your-own-honey-you'll-be-a-heap-by-the-side-of-the-road version. (The heap was stage three, wishing for the transporter beams to come and plop our weary bodies where we needed to get to, to have a cool drink and bathe and rest.) So, I think that letting go, mile after mile and day after day, might have helped me to notice the veil parting just a little bit, for just a moment, to reveal a Unity that is true all the time, radiating throughout our cosmos.

Or perhaps it was what they call grace, a gifted moment. Who knows? This sort of thing might sound highly improbable—it doesn't happen very often. But it's not because I was special in any way. In my deepest heart as a scientist, I know there is something special about *all* of us, and about this mysterious world we find wrapped around ourselves. Most of the time we think that science affirms that everything in the world can be known, but it actually doesn't do that at all. We generally move and act within a certain sphere where things seem completely knowable and predictable, but this is just a subset of our marvelous universe. It's almost as though we and our lives are in a huge, magnificent castle but we're in a tiny corner of it, gazing into the wall and oblivious to everything else. As we gentle ourselves, relax, and be willing to see with something other than our forward-gazing eyes, we can sense into our being as part of the huge castle and all that surrounds it.

Letting go (*kenosis*) leads to abundance

Jesus gave hints on how humans can participate more deeply in exchange with this Unity, and with the Wholeness within each other. In addition to "Love your neighbor as yourself," he said "Give and it will be given to you in good measure, pressed down and overflowing, they shall cast into your lap. For with what measure you measure it will be measured to you" (Luke 6:38, Aramaic Bible in Plain English). The words in that phrase that catch me are "pressed down and overflowing." This invokes an exchange where our open-handed letting go (sometimes described with the Greek word *kenosis*), is key to receiving the abundance of the cosmic web, the fully loving field of mercy that always surrounds and interpenetrates our world. Jesus also gave hints on how *not* to notice: he cautioned about grasping or hoarding; for example, in the parable of a merchant who was so excited to be building new barns to store all his goods, but who died that very night. He told a parable of the talents (a type of monetary unit), praising those who invested their talents and got return on them, chastising the person who buried the talents he was given—even though that person did it to save and preserve them. He encouraged people to get into the game, to fully participate and offer the world what they have, what they *are*, rather than to clench up and hoard.

The stance of hoarding, of clenching up, closes up the heart and the faculties that connect the mystery of our humanness to this great stream of life. It turns out that it also changes our physiology, in particular a mechanism in our nervous system that evolved to help us connect with each other, to participate in this great flowing exchange.

Evolution prioritizes exchange in social relationships

When we hoard, or clench up, certain parts of our brain are closed off and the amygdala, the base of fear and anxiety, dominates. When we grasp, tense up, and hold on tight to protect what we think we need for our own survival, we disengage a system that evolved in humans over time called the "ventral vagal complex." This feature in the autonomic nervous system helps us override anger and aggression, and give and respond to cues that help us calm each other down. This restores regulation in our nervous system, and greatly enhances social relationships vital to our survival, prioritizing positive, stabilizing exchanges among people.[64] In other words, we have evolved a capacity that encourages us to trust and offer ourselves to the greater good of the group rather than focus on just our own needs or reactivity.

In research conducted at the Traumatic Stress Research Consortium at Indiana University, scientists studying this complex found that a good indicator of the healthy functioning of this regulatory complex is the entrainment of the heart and brain. This can be measured with "respiratory sinus arrhythmia" or the heart rate variation (HRV) as we breathe in and out.[65] A higher HRV (which can be measured at least roughly by personal fitness devices) indicates that the ventral vagal system is operating, helping our body to act in a more integrated fashion. A lower HRV is correlated with stress, perception of threat, or clenching. And this mechanism is an exchange: the researchers found that people who are rooted in a sense of integrated being can ground others with a sense of calm radiating from their voices, from their presence. This can reinforce the ventral vagal complex in others, increasing the entrainment of the heart and brain. Overall, the evolution of this complex would enhance the potential for integration within each person, and more importantly, the cohesiveness of the group and their joint survival—even their thriving!

The whole is greater than the sum of its parts

This concept of individuals coming together in a synergistic way is not unique to humans. As we mentioned earlier, over long periods of time atoms joined to make molecules, molecules miraculously assembled to make cells, and cells joined to form organisms. These are exchange-based processes as well. When two atoms come together to make a molecule, their electron clouds come together and become shared among the two nuclei. This sharing is a win-win: the energy is lowered and they become more stable, and new properties emerge that would be difficult to imagine from the two separate atoms. The cores of the atoms are still the same and they retain their unique identities, but they are part of a new, greater, shared whole. When molecules react together the process becomes even more complex: their shared electron clouds (or molecular orbitals) have geometric shapes, often with uneven charge and polarity, so that they need to come together in a particular way or they won't react. The more molecules you have gathered together and the more energy they have, the more likely they will come together aligned in such a way that they can react to form something new, with entirely new properties.

This reminds me of a principle that Catholic priest and scientist Pierre Teilhard de Chardin laid out, especially in *The Human Phenomenon*.[66] As a paleontologist, he studied evolution in many species and noticed that as species "fan out" geographically into new environments, those with certain mutations that can adapt to the local conditions will thrive, over time resulting in sub-species with different characteristics. Yet, just as molecules gathered more closely together may be more likely to react, humans, he noted, even in their spreading out over the globe, have been contained by the finite shape of our earth, which continues to bring us back together. This allows tendrils of the fan to reconnect, to *coalesce*. He even asserted that the coalescence occurring, where close grouping brings diverse individuals together, is the ultimate fate of evolution: just as the meridians of the globe merge at a pole then spread out along the equator and merge again at the opposite pole. He also said, based on his many observations, that the bringing together of units in confined spaces (such as humans on our earth, or organisms confined to a particular environment) makes it more likely that they will evolve into more complex structures.

My granddaughter recently found a sea pickle on the beach. This structure is actually thousands of tiny multicellular organisms joined in a colony in a tubular shape. As ocean water flows through this tube, the organisms all have access to the phytoplankton they consume as food, and the flow through the tube also helps propel the colony through the water to find new food. The new whole is definitely greater than the sum of its parts!

We find that as coalescence results in new organisms with new properties, for example the cell from molecules, organisms from cells, and the evolution of more complex organisms, greater consciousness evolves. Teilhard de Chardin was onto this way before the neuroscientists! He described evolution as headed from a self-centered focus on our own survival as *individuals* (or our own family or tribe) toward a more coherent participation in a world as *persons*. Each person contributes as a unique human, but attuned to the greater good, willing to set aside their personal agenda. Persons acknowledge their relationship within a dynamic shared field of mercy. They are also aware of their responsibility to each other, and to our planet home. We are being invited to jump whole-heartedly into this shared field, contributing the talents given to us and synergistically multiplying them as we join in the cosmic dance.

Letting go to a greater whole: The kingdom of heaven

If we take this context and look back at what Jesus was saying, about loving your neighbor as yourself, and "I am in my father, and you in me, and I in you" (John 14:20, NRSV), we can see that he was pointing to a highly relational web. At the heart of this is kenosis, or letting go, of our usual self-centered desires and preoccupation with random A influences, to emphasize our evolutionary propensity towards the greater good. He was calling us to a greater whole, that he often called the kingdom of heaven, assuring us that it is at hand, or within us. It is hard for us to predict what this whole might be like, but that is inherent in the kenotic process—it involves deep trust and relaxation that comes from letting go, even of thinking we need to do something to achieve this. It is in relaxing into the wholeness, the kingdom that is already here, within and among us, that we accept the invitation.

Jesus gave so many analogies for what the very present kingdom of heaven is like. For one thing it is like a mustard seed: a tiny speck that grows in the middle of anything, yet keeps its own character, and expands into a bush where birds can nest. This kingdom is also highly inclusive: a king throws a wedding for his son, but because of conflicting priorities (A influences!) none of the invited guests accept the invitation, and he sends his servants out into the streets to invite everyone they find. It is highly participational, relational, and the exact opposite of building our own barns. It is a kingdom of love, compassion, of full participation in a dynamic field of mercy and mutual nurturing, where cosmic assistance is always available.

Our bodies can give us a huge clue as to when we are on track: as we let go of our hoarding, our clenching, the body relaxes. It's only in a relaxed state that we can be in tune with the cosmic web. You can take a step in that direction right now: notice where you might be holding tension in your body and sink into it, feeling the sensation of your feet, legs, belly, shoulders, and relax into *the way it actually feels in this moment right now*, without needing to change it. What is your experience of this? Even if you don't sense anything, just be with that too. We all know from personal experience how letting go is much easier when we love and trust. Just as scientists showed that people can calm each other with their voice and quality of presence and help each other to restore heart/brain entrainment, letting go is easier given a sense of safe space.

Opening to Love: Learning to forgive and to receive

I understand the wounds that have not healed in you. They exist
because God and Love have yet to become real enough to allow you
to forgive the dream. You still listen to an old alley song that brings
your body pain; now chain your ears to His pacing drum and flute.
Fix your eyes upon the magnificent arch of His brow that supports
and allows this universe to expand. Your hands, feet, and heart are
wise and want to know the warmth of a Perfect One's circle.

—Hafiz[67]

I read a news story one day, about a young boy who didn't have even basic things in his birth home—a bed, food in the cabinets, or baths. He had been in several foster homes and had finally found an adoptive home. In the first couple of years at his new home he would destroy any gifts that were given to him—he didn't think he deserved them.

I started to weep as I read this story. I could see that my own dear love, the One who loves all dearly, was constantly offering their hand and I had pushed it away, more times than I could ever know. I could feel the heartbreak of it—such an amazing, precious gift refused. This is echoed in the words of sixteenth century Christian mystic Teresa of Ávila: "A thousand souls hear His call every second, but most everyone then looks into their life's mirror and says, 'I am not worthy to leave this sadness.'"[68]

Each of us, whether with extensive trauma or even just the basic survival structure we build as part of working our way through this world, has our own reasons for turning away from this huge relational field of being, of compassion. Perhaps we feel inadequate, or find ourselves caught up in frantic busy-ness, unable to see the value of slowing down to make room for awe or wonder. Or, maybe we fear that if we yield to the sense of a Source of Being, we'll lose our sense of control. The part of us that wants to be in control, that thinks it is in control, has no idea how to participate fully in this radiant divine exchange.

So often we rush to give, to try and give love, but without also receiving we can find ourselves overextended and drained. Even the word "love" can be pretty loaded for people, and it can be associated with certain expectations in return for what we offer to others. Sometimes Buddhists use the term "LovingKindness" instead, because it is without expectation of return—it is offered freely, without any draining or loss on our part, because ultimately it doesn't come from us—it is more like aligning with the cosmic field of mercy we are talking about.

Opening to mercy

As Teresa of Ávila said later in that same poem, "He sang again, a song even sweeter ... 'I made you dear, and all I make is perfect. Please come close, for I desire you.'"[69] I would like to open up this word "perfect" with an Aramaic lens. Jesus uses the same word in Matthew 5:48 (NRSV), often translated as "Be perfect, therefore, as your heavenly Father is perfect." The root, *gemar*, also means to complete, to mature. And in the passive participle[70] form we find in this verse, it can mean that we are *being* perfected, completed; that it is a process we can offer ourselves up to. Either way, this verse can be interpreted that we are being called to this completion, this molding of our being, to reveal the inner perfection we always had, from the beginning. It's a matter of letting go; a matter of *kenosis*.

How can we begin to accept that we can open to this Sacred Unity, to offer ourselves to the divine hand that is always completing us, revealing the perfection in which we were made, in a loving field of mercy? Can we receive as well as give in this beautiful exchange? It may not be our first instinct to openly receive, yet as we learn to let go and embrace, we can become like a chalice for the abundant mercy that is being offered.

This can start with the kind of welcoming we just talked about, sinking into this moment as it is, into our bodies and our emotions exactly as we find them. It is a fully-embodied, physically relaxed presence, related to mindfulness. It's almost as though the part of us that can truly receive is aligned with this flowing web of exchange, and knows itself as fully at home, even *incarnated*, there. The alchemy of this is transformative for our being. As we let go and offer what we truly are,

58

willing to fully inhabit even those moments that feel difficult and from which we want to turn away, it may not change circumstances at all, but it changes the way we experience them, with our presence of being. We align with the abundant field and receive its gifts, in the midst of where we find ourselves.

The gifts can flow out freely through us into the world without effort or loss, in a beautiful, even divine, exchange. Our cup may so abundantly overflow that it simultaneously flows out in giving, without any effort, as the Beatitude promises: "Blessed are the merciful, for they *are receiving* mercy." When we truly receive, we can become transmitters of love and other precious qualities such as joy, peace, forbearance, kindness, goodness, faithfulness, gentleness, and self-control. The possibilities are powerful. Teilhard de Chardin wrote: "Someday, after mastering the winds, the waves, the tides and gravity, we shall harness for God the energies of love, and then, for the second time in the history of the world, man will have discovered fire."[71]

Questions for reflection:

- Take a moment to pause and connect with your breathing. Notice any tension you are holding and sink into it, noticing its qualities. Also note any emotions you might feel as you do this. As you sink into this moment, exactly as it is, in what ways are you participating in exchanges with the world around—with other people or with animals or other elements of nature?

- Consider that you are intimately related with stars, that you are made of stardust—does it broaden your view of who you are and how you are connected with the universe?

- Recall in your life an experience of the type of mercy, or LovingKindness we have been talking about, that flows into or out of you spontaneously without any expectation of return. What was that like to experience—how did it feel in your body? What helped you to receive and/or offer it? How does it feel now, to recall it?

Chapter 7

Red Shift Cosmology vs. Oneness of the Field

Spirit is the higher state of matter.... Matter is the matrix of consciousness and all around us consciousness, born of matter, is constantly advancing towards some ultra-human.
—**Pierre Teilhard de Chardin, in** *The Heart of Matter*

In contrast with the view of Divine Exchange, which is consistent with the connection shown in modern physics, many of the world's major religions take a more binary view, categorizing things as good/bad, yin/yang, higher/lower. The perennial philosophy, or *sophia perennis*, that subtly underlies these religions often implies that there is some high-energy source (perhaps a heaven "out there") and we poor humans are removed or "fallen" from the source. In the *sophia perennis* models, there is a great shift between the spiritual and material realms: creation of matter is often seen as a fall, or an exile from the source of origin. And humans, being made of matter, have a long way to go, a steep ladder to climb, to reach this heaven that supposedly lies outside of us.

In *The Holy Trinity and the Law of Three*, Cynthia Bourgeault calls these *sophia perennis* models "red-shift" maps, in the sense of the Doppler shift you might hear as an ambulance goes by. As the siren approaches, the relative energy emitted by the siren increases and the sound frequency you hear is higher. This is called a "blue shift" because blue light is on the higher energy side of visible light. As the sound moves away from you the siren sounds lower to you as the relative frequency, or energy, decreases. This is called a red shift because the pitch you hear (and the energy) are lowered, and red light is on the lower energy side of visible light.

How do we reconcile this red-shift cosmology that permeates many of the world's major religions with the highly interpenetrated messages in Jesus' teachings, such as "You are in me and I am in you" and "The Kingdom of Heaven is *within* you, at hand"? Our current twenty-first century cosmology provides a better lens to view them, in contrast to the prevailing paradigms in Jesus' time. Many older paradigms are still inherent in our world, but we are beginning to see through them as new physics emerges and creates a crack in vessels of tradition so that the brilliant light of the cosmos can't help but begin to shine through everything.

Matter as coiled energy ($E = mc^2$)

There's just no way around this one: YOU MATTER, unless you multiply yourself by the speed of light squared. Then YOU ENERGY.

—Neil deGrasse Tyson

Let's start with matter itself. When we examine it more closely, we see that it is not inferior, or even separate, from something loftier and more spiritual—it's far more amazing than that. In fact, matter exists more as a localized pattern of energy than a solid ball. You are likely familiar with Einstein's famous equation showing that energy (E) can be converted to mass (m), and vice versa in a dynamic interplay, or exchange. When you multiply mass by the speed of light (about 22,000 times the speed of a jet plane) squared, c^2, you figure out how much energy is condensed in that matter—it's an unfathomable amount! The exchange also flows the other way: the greater energy you have available, the greater the mass you can produce. Particle accelerators such as the Large Hadron

Collider (LHC) located near Geneva, Switzerland collide particles with such high energy that new particles, such as the Higgs boson, [72] are created from the energy.

Going back the other way again, mass can release a huge amount of energy: Einstein's equation tells us that if we could somehow convert one gram of mass, about half the size of an American dime, entirely to energy, it would produce enough to run a one hundred fifty watt television or other device for nineteen thousand years![73] The sheer scale of energy that can be released from mass is the basis for nuclear energy power plants.

Light is unique in that it lies outside of spacetime. Einstein's special theory of relativity tells us that the faster we go, approaching the speed of light, time slows down and space shrinks. If I went on a journey on a space ship at speeds approaching the speed of light, I could actually come back younger than my younger sisters who have aged, because time slows down for me at those speeds.

The Body of Light

In humans, the exchange between material body tissue and light energy is a mystical phenomenon. This is not the same phenomenon described by Einstein, but the exchange of matter and energy bring it to mind.

According to some Eastern religious traditions, including Tibetan Buddhism and Taoism, highly realized human beings (who have fully realized the perfection of our true nature) can accomplish the "body of light" in which living tissue of the body undergoes transmutation to light energy over several days. One of my teachers described watching his master go through this. As the master approached the end of his life, he requested that he be sewn into a tent and not disturbed for a week. Over the next days, his students observed bright light streaming from cracks in the tent. When they opened the tent after the light had subsided there was no trace of the master's body; only the hair and nails, the non-living tissue from the body, remained. There are many stories of this in the Tibetan Buddhist tradition as well. For example, living Dzogchen master Chögyal Namkhai Norbu (b. 1938) says that his uncle, Togden Ugyen Tendzin, achieved the body of light, witnessed in shock by the officers who were imprisoning him.

I don't know of any scientific study that has documented a phenomenon of emission of bright light from a human body.[74] But I mention it as a mystery here. In the Eastern traditions, when a spiritual master realizes the body of light, they are understood to consciously exit our 4D spacetime and they can step back in at any time or place, embodied or not, to assist living beings. Thich Nhat Hanh, for example, said that the Buddha continued to be with people in the Dharma body, teaching and guiding. He was referring to a fully perfected form of the body that exists outside of spacetime, that is beyond circumstance. In the Wisdom traditions, we are encouraged to build vehicles, forms of being that can navigate the more subtle realms unseen to the eye, beyond our usual spacetime. I will refer more to these realms soon, as they are called to mind by the multidimensionality of the science that unfolds later in this chapter.

Did Jesus achieve the Body of Light?

I also wonder about the connection of the body of light with the story of Jesus' body disappearing from the sealed tomb, and his reappearance over the next few weeks to his disciples. His reappearance was in a different form: his disciples did not always recognize him right away. He was said to pass through walls, and to mysteriously appear and disappear at will. On the shroud of Turin, a fourteen-foot cloth thought by some to be the burial cloth of Jesus, an image appears that could have been created by bright light. The image on the shroud, tinged with blood, is of a Semitic man who was crucified (with arms above him in a Y shape), and with wounds that correspond to the description of Jesus' wounds in the Gospels.[75] Some scientists were able to recreate a similar image using ultraviolet light.[76] It remains an intriguing mystery.

I also wonder about the reports of appearances of Jesus' mother Mary in places such as Lourdes in France and Tepeyac hill near Mexico

City, where the Virgin of Guadalupe appeared, and also the intimate feelings of presence that so many spiritual seekers have experienced from a master who has passed on, with whom they feel a deep continuing relationship. The message is usually one of love, of presence, of assistance, and sometimes an urgent message regarding something we might bring forth in the world around us.

I have felt a very real, yet human presence myself, from spiritual beings no longer in the flesh as we know it. For example, in the House of Mary outside of Ephesus, thought to be the place where Jesus' mother Mary lived out her days, I felt a palpable, coherent immanence, radiating with the sense of an emergence of something new and unimaginably loving. There was a deep sense of assurance: that things are okay, and that they will be okay. I felt entranced by it, as though I wanted to stay there with her, even as my traveling companions were urging me to come out. The kind of presence I felt in the House of Mary reminded me of the sense I get when sitting in a room with an experienced meditator who is deeply immersed in practice. There is sometimes a bright, alert vibrancy that extends throughout the room. I felt a similar kind of presence in the House of Mary, and continue to feel her guiding presence in prayer, as many others do.

These kinds of visions are sometimes vivid, and likely to appear more inwardly to the receiver, visible only to the heart (our integrated organ of spiritual perception). I will say more about that later, but here I would like to further explore the exchange of energy in physics, where scientists can create particles, for example photons, out of the vast field of what physicists call the vacuum.[77] The vacuum isn't really empty, as the name implies, but is a vast and dynamic field of possibility where local fluctuations in energy can give rise to particles. Let there be light!

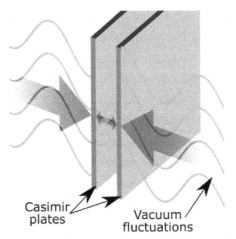

Let there be light! Drawing of an experiment used to create photons from the vacuum.
Source: Emok, CC BY-SA 3.0 <https://creativecommons.org/licenses/by-sa/3.0>, via Wikimedia Commons.

High-energy collisions and other interactions can also give rise to particles, and sometimes what are called virtual particles, that have measurable effects. Heisenberg's uncertainty principle can account for this last case.

A dynamic field of creativity: Heisenberg and exchange

In modern physics, there is no such thing as "nothing." Even in a perfect vacuum, pairs of virtual particles are constantly being created and destroyed. The existence of these particles is no mathematical fiction. Though they cannot be directly observed, the effects they create are quite real. The assumption that they exist leads to predictions that have been confirmed by experiment to a high degree of accuracy.
—**Richard Morris,** in *The Edges of Science*

Earlier I mentioned the flagrant abundance and creative flow of exchange and interabiding Oneness in the field of Mercy. For me, it is reminiscent of Werner Heisenberg's uncertainty principle, especially as it invokes Einstein's interchange of matter and energy on a tiny scale. The uncertainty principle is one of the most abused, misunderstood concepts in physics, being used to explain all sorts of phenomena by nonscientists. But it does describe the basis for a magnificent creative and dynamic exchange underlying our universe.

According to the uncertainty principle,[78] if you know where a particle is, you don't know its momentum, and vice versa. Therefore as the space scale gets very small, momentum becomes quite uncertain, and energy also fluctuates with big spikes. The more we might try to pin down a particle in space, the more wildly unpredictable the energy would get! And we just learned that energy and mass are interchangeable. So, as energy fluctuates on the tiny sub-quantum scale, virtual particles can spontaneously appear and disappear, as energy and mass are inter-exchanged. Physicists call this a type of "creation and annihilation."[79] The first time my quantum mechanics professor mentioned this astonishing process, I thought for sure that we had crossed the line into science fiction!

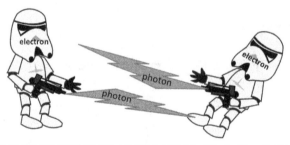

Two electrons are repelled by the creation of "virtual" photons that act as "messenger" particles, causing the electrons to move away from each other. (J. Andrews Hayter)

The energy-mass exchange occurs any time two particles interact. Two electrons are repelled (think of the opposing ends of two magnets repelling each other), for example, because they shoot virtual photons at each other, pushing them apart. The virtual photons act as "messengers" that result in the two electrons repelling each other. This works somewhat similarly to how you would move backwards if you were standing on a skateboard and threw a heavy rock off of it. The electrons move apart from each other as they "create" and throw off "virtual" photons, and then the photons disappear again.[80] This was surprising to me! Even though atoms are mostly empty space, electrons tend to avoid each other, causing atoms to act as though they are solid. This enables us to move atoms (and molecules) around because of the mutually-re-pelling electron clouds surrounding them. But we could also imagine it as a sparring match with the electrons grabbing particles out of the air to throw at each other, like a big snow ball fight.

The virtual photons we are talking about emerge from what phys-icists call "the vacuum." The vacuum isn't really empty, as the name implies, but is a vast and dynamic field of possibility where local fluc-tuations in energy can give rise to these virtual particles.[81] This doesn't just happen on the tiny scale where electrons have their snowball fight: scientists have created real pairs of photons from the vacuum in the lab,[82] the emergence of something from nothing. Let there be light!

The dynamic, creative field is also highly inter-relational. Quantum field theory also extends our concept of exchange and relationship, and even of wave functions (remember Psi?) across the entire universe (or multiverse!), resulting in an intimate entanglement of all things.

Everything is entangled with everything else

Entanglement is the secret ingredient.
—Sean Carroll[83]

In contrast with models of diminishment with distance from a source outside of ourselves, in Quantum Field Theory we will see that every-thing is somehow entangled with everything else: every particle arises, more like a shimmering, from infinite fields spanning the universe. As a rough understanding of what a field is, we encounter classical fields in everyday life: the air pressure around you right now, for example, is a field. Our bodies also emit fields, measureable, for example, with EEGs of the brain and EKGs of the heart.

In quantum field theory every "point" in space is part of one vast inter-connected quantum wave. These quantum fields indicate that everything in the universe is far more connected than we usually perceive or acknowledge, in an intimately interwoven universe where each point is in relationship with all the others.

The matter we are made of doesn't just appear from nowhere: quantum fields bring into being all the stuff we daily encounter. All types of matter or force, including fermions such as electrons and quarks (that form protons and neutrons, for example), and bosons such as photons of light, as well as gravity, arise from vast, connected, dynamic fields that extend throughout the universe. Every type of particle arises from its field: electrons from an electron field, quarks from a quark field, etc. Every single electron in the universe, for example, arises from excitations in the electron field, less like a particle and more like a localized energetic vibration of the field. Quantum field theory (QFT) describes these fields.[84]

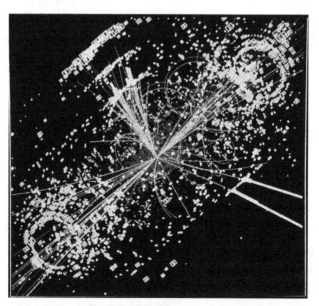

Experimental data from the LHC at CERN shows decay of the Higgs boson to form 4 muons, another type of particle (they are fermions). The Higgs boson arises from the Higgs quantum field.
Source: https://simple.wikipedia.org/wiki/Higgs_field.

Abundance in action: A potent field of creative energy

One of the many quantum fields is the Higgs field. Full of energy, creative, and hyper-connected, it is sometimes called the "Big Mama" of all fields: it leads to all the other forces and fields in the universe.[85] The Higgs field is infinitely rich in energy: each miniscule point in the field contains energy that can be converted to mass as particles swim through the field. The Higgs field gives rise to the Higgs boson, observed in 2012 at the LHC in Switzerland. Thus, we have evidence for a field spanning the entire universe, containing all other fields and forces, and bringing the mass of the fundamental particles (electrons and quarks) we are made of into being. No wonder the Higgs has been awe-inspiring to so many. I highly recommend (even though the dancing is terrible and people don't really wear lab coats at the LHC) the video, *The LHC Rap: Understanding the Higgs Boson*.[86] About the Higgs, it goes:

> But the Higgs – I still haven't said just what it does.
> They suppose that particles have mass because
> There is this Higgs field that extends through all space
> And some particles slow down while other particles race
> Straight through, like the photon, it has no mass.
> But something heavy, like the top quark, is dragging its ass!
> And the Higgs is a boson that carries a force,
> And makes particles take orders from the field that is its source.

A vast creative symphony

Form is Emptiness and Emptiness is Form
—The Heart Sutra[87]

With QFT, we continue to see that matter is not inferior—it is rich, imbued with energy, and highly enmeshed within a creative relational web, poetically reminiscent of the "field of mercy" described earlier.

Our idea of solidity, or of independent existence of anything, disappears even further—even the "solid" tiny nucleus at the center of an atom is more like a collection of excited energy vibrations than a solid mass.[88]

Here, any sense of separation or red shift disappears entirely. Our relational cosmic web arises again: *we can't separate our notion of a particle from the energy-rich space that surrounds it.* And particles are constantly being created and destroyed from a vacuum of abundant creativity. In other words, empty space is not empty at all: this constant vibrant dance even makes the fields stable.[89] This quantum field perspective gives even more dimension to the Buddhist Heart Sutra.

The phenomena of creation and annihilation bring about the forces we see, for example, the repulsion of two negative charges. The photon-shooting electrons we saw earlier take on a slightly different tune: we could now say that "a vibration in the electron field causes a vibration in the photon field, which then interacts with another vibration in the electron field." Although that's a mouthful, these relational vibrations start to sound like one great creative symphony! It's almost like a dynamic underlying dance of the universe, pulsating and bringing life to it, reminiscent of the Hindu god Shiva, whose dance of creation of the new and destruction of what is no longer essential is said to keep the universe in motion.

More music of the spheres: String theory

There is an additional level of joy for me, and even playfulness that dances into our many possibilities and cosmic web connections when we introduce String Theory and M-Theory. As we unravel them a bit you might sense the wonder that many physicists have as they uncover more about our cosmos. These theories became useful in addressing a great unanswered question in physics that was relevant as scientists studied the first moments after the Big Bang: how could we even begin to talk about an immeasurably huge amount of mass (and supposedly an unfathomable amount of gravity) arising from a tiny (quantum scale and smaller) space? For one thing, time has no meaning on these scales, so it's tough to even talk about a beginning when we are talking about timeless time. Recall that Heisenberg's uncertainty principle says all bets are off about energy when space is so tiny. And Einstein's general relativity (the field theory of gravitation), which accounts for very large scales such as our universe, was incompatible with quantum theory, which as we've seen accounts for very small things on the size of atoms and below. In other words, QFT did not account for gravity.

String theory, which first emerged in the late 1960s, is one candidate for the elusive "Theory of Everything"[90] that Einstein struggled with, as it works toward reconciling quantum mechanics with gravity. There is controversy about string theory, with enthusiastic support from prominent physicists including Edward Witten, Michio Kaku, and Stephen Hawking.[91] But the question remains open: there are also alternate theories, including "quantum gravity," that attempt to unify gravity and quantum mechanics. Physicist Sabine Hossenfelder, who spent much time turning over and comparing the ideas of various physicists, wrote in support of string theory: "But for all the controversy that surrounds string theory in the public sphere, within the physics community few doubt its use.... The mathematics of string theory is deeply rooted in theories that demonstrably describe nature: quantum field theory and general relativity ... But whether string theory really is the sought-after theory of quantum gravity ... we still don't know."[92]

Despite what we may still not know, string theory is worth looking into. It says that all of the elementary particles we have been talking about are vibrations of tiny one-dimensional strings. These strings help stretch out distances on the Planck scale[93] from point particles to tiny one-dimensional strings that look like particles. By enlarging the scale a bit, it makes gravity more compatible with quantum theory.

Stringing it all together

In string theory we of course have the music of strings which gives us the particles we see in nature.
—Michio Kaku

I mean, give me a guitar, give me a piano, give me a broom and string, I wouldn't get bored anywhere.
—Keith Richards

Imagine that you were holding a piece of string in your two hands, and vibrating it up and down. If you did it quickly, the area over where it was vibrating might begin to appear solid. That is somewhat analogous to what strings are thought to be capable of, to create all the observed particles of what physicists call the "standard model."

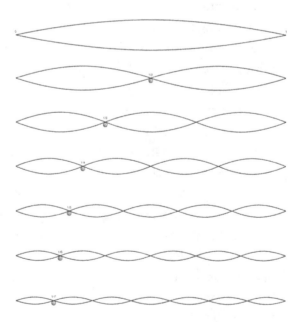

Resonant frequencies of a guitar string, from the fundamental (top) to higher harmonics (increasing down the image). The shorter the wavelength (distance between 2 peaks or troughs in the wave), the higher frequency we hear.
Source: Public domain, via Wikimedia Commons.

If you've ever watched a stringed instrument being tuned you might notice that as the player tightens the string it plays a higher frequency, which we hear as a higher note (see resonant frequencies in a string above). As the player places their fingers on the strings the wavelength (distance from peak to peak) varies, and the string can sound out different notes. And the longer or thicker the vibrating string, the lower the note we hear. In an analogous way, scientists have shown that the tension and resonance energy of the miniscule one-dimensional strings in string theory could give rise to all the particles and forces that physicists are aware of, as well as predicting some new ones that have not yet been observed. (It would require extremely powerful particle accelerators to observe them.)

String theory is still under development: several entirely different versions of it have been conceived, and we have yet to observe some of the new particles it predicts. However, M-theory, a quantum theory in (at least) eleven dimensions, promisingly brings together all of these different forms of string theory under one mother theory. This theory invokes Oneness in a highly interwoven, interdependent reality.

The letter M in M-theory is said to represent magic, mystery,[94] or membrane.[95] Or perhaps it could be music, or mother! Physicist Michio Kaku says:

> The music of these membranes is subatomic particles. Each subatomic particle represents a note on a vibrating string. So, believe it or not, we now have a candidate for the "mind of God" that Albert Einstein wrote about over the last thirty years of his life. The mind of God, in this picture, would be cosmic music, resonating throughout eleven-dimensional hyperspace.[96]

The strings (or loops, in some cases, or even membranes) of M-theory are strange entities: they have been calculated to exist in many more dimensions than the usual four spacetime dimensions in which we are aware of navigating our lives. M-theory, called the "Mother of all String Theories" by Kaku, proposes eleven dimensions: the three large spatial dimensions we are used to, plus time, and seven additional very tiny spatial hyper-dimensions that are curled up onto each point in space. In this theory any point in our three-dimensional space could be called a "brane," with many higher dimensions associated with it.

One representation of a multi-dimensional (Calabi-Yau) space.
Source: Andrew J. Hanson, Indiana University, CC BY-SA 3.0 <https://creativecommons.org/licenses/by-sa/3.0>, via Wikimedia Commons.

The tiny spatial dimensions are difficult to visualize (but they have been modeled mathematically, see above for an example).[97] Even though these dimensions are very small (the relative size of the Planck scale to a single atom is about the same as the relative size of a person to the *entire universe* with all its galaxies), they could still affect reality as we perceive it.

To get an idea of how a tiny dimension can be significant, imagine an ant in a one-dimensional world[98] walking along the 1D line, the only path that is available to it in this dimension. If the ant meets another ant, each would see just the front face of the other ant as a spot, and they would not be able to pass each other. But if we add to this picture a second rolled up dimension, however small, the possibilities increase greatly as the ant's 1D world becomes a 2D world.[99] The ant could crawl along this cylindrical shape as though along the outside of a garden hose and could thus walk past the other ant, something it could not do if only the single dimension existed.

This thin tube might appear only one-dimensional when viewed from a distance, much as a power wire might appear to us viewed from a distance. In a similar way, in our four-dimensional world of three very large spatial dimensions plus time, the other seven spatial dimensions may not be obvious at all because they are very small in comparison, but they could affect the behavior of particles that could utilize these dimensions.

Spider's web after rain.
Source: Image by Светлана (Svetlana) from Pixabay Public Domain,
via Creative Commons.

The Luminous Web

There are some mind-blowing implications when you bring in higher dimensions, invoking a highly intimate relationship among all things. Barbara Brown Taylor used the term "Luminous Web" to describe the sense of energy, creativity, and connectedness she saw in the quantum fields and hyperdimensions.[100] I'll continue along those lines with an analogy that might help to visualize how this world of M-theory might connect things that seem unrelated. These multidimensional "portals" at each point in space are reminiscent of what a spider's web might look like after a rain. With small drops of water at each point, shining in the bright morning sun, we could imagine each drop reflecting all the others. And each reflecting drop would be reflected in all the others. In a hyper-dimensional space, there would be an intimate relationship among all the points: each point would actually contain all the others. In a sense, you could call this holographic. (A holographic image, for example, is different from a typical photographic image in that, if you cut a photo in half, you lose half of the picture. But in a hologram each point contains light from the entire object: even if you cut it in half, you would still see the whole image, just with lower resolution.) In a holographic universe, each point would contain all the information, *all* of us, and all points in "time."

This unique hyper-dimensional, intimately inter-related field was hinted at many centuries ago as Indra's net, a concept in Hinduism (the Atharva Veda, c. 1000 BCE) and Chinese Buddhism. Philosopher Francis Cook's description may help you to visualize it. He wrote:

> Far away in the heavenly abode of the great god Indra, there is a wonderful net which has been hung by some cunning artificer in such a manner that it stretches out infinitely in all directions. In accordance with the extravagant tastes of deities, the artificer has hung a single glittering jewel in each "eye" of the net, and since the net itself is infinite in dimension, the jewels are infinite in number. There hang the jewels, glittering "like" stars in the first magnitude, a wonderful sight to behold. If we now arbitrarily select one of these jewels for inspection and look closely at it, we will discover that in its polished surface there are reflected all the other jewels in the net, infinite in number. Not only that, but each of the jewels reflected in this one jewel is also reflecting all the other jewels, so that there is an infinite reflecting process occurring.[101]

The infinite reflection of each "jewel" in Indra's net is evocative of the sparkling drops of rain in the spider's web, or the mathematical hyper-dimensional spaces of M-theory. If each point is indeed a portal into seven additional spatial dimensions, *there would be no separation between each of these points,* a concept intuited by Chinese and other contemplatives. And even if M-theory turned out not to be correct, quantum field theory, which has been shown to be correct in many areas, poses a deep entanglement across the universe, potentially in one single wave function containing everything in the universe, including all of us. Essentially, we are all connected.

If we poetically extrapolate back to our discussion of Wisdom vs. *sophia perennis* traditions as viewed from this cosmology, we find no red shift: in this hyper-dimensional interwoven universe there would be no separation between God and humans, or humans from each other. Jesus' interabiding words begin to make more sense here: "I am in my Father, and you are in me, and I am in you."[102] His echoes of interabiding Oneness fit far better into our current cosmology of highly entangled quantum fields and the infinitely reflecting holographic web of M-theory than in the old model of a flat earth, with earth here and heaven out there somewhere, that prevailed during his time. And his call for us to love one another also fits here, especially as we abide together in this field of lovingkindness, in the arms of a loving mercy, receiving and offering it to one another. And if the universe is holographic and each point, or each of us, is a fractal, a complete pattern within a larger pattern of the whole, then as we learn to coalesce or to come together in a coherent way, as proposed by Teilhard, the overall holographic "picture" comes into better resolution. With the thought of more of us coming together for a common good, I start to wonder what the human equivalent of a sea pickle colony would look like!

Meanwhile let's explore a few more implications of a hyperdimensional universe, and what it means for interconnections among all things.

To the fifth dimension and beyond!

The idea of ten dimensions might sound exciting, but they would cause real problems if you forgot where you parked your car.
—**Stephen Hawking, in** *The Grand Design*

The existence of dimensions beyond the usual four-dimensional space-time can mean that connections not apparent from our three-dimensional spatial view may be affecting us, and our relationship with reality. Imagine that you were a flatland creature confined just to this 2D page that you are reading. If a 3D cat started to walk across the page you lived on, you would only see minor parts of it. You might see the edges of round flat objects like circles appear where its paws touched the page, and then see them magically disappear as the cat lifted its foot for the next step.

Any 2D creatures could find their view of the paw spots blocked by other 2D beings, or by 3D objects standing between them and the cat paws. However, the cat, as a 3D creature, could see all of the 2D page at once—the full 2D world. From the 2D flatland perspective, the extra dimension available to the cat could make it seem like it had magical powers of disappearing or appearing from nowhere, or seeing through walls or over large distances. The cat's three dimensions could cause things in 2D flatland to appear correlated (e.g. some paw spots moving simultaneously, or if some appear, they all tend to appear at about the same time), even though they may seem to be autonomous in the two-dimensional Flatland.

I also wonder about our 2D creature and what would happen if they sunk their experience into the whole sheet of paper in a type of non-judging presence. Might they sense the movement of the cat upon it, even if they couldn't see it with the eyes that could perceive only what is right in front of them? As a rough analogy, imagine you were lying under a sheet with eyes closed, and you felt a cat walking over you. As you felt each paw exert pressure and then lift, you would sense that these movements were not separate events, but part of a larger pattern.

Of course, your previous 3D experience of the cat reinforces this, but even without that, if you were a flatland creature you might be able to sense this connection.

As I recall some odd quantum properties such as the wave/particle duality and entanglement, I wonder whether they start to make more sense when we consider hyper-dimensions, or spatial dimensions in addition to the three large dimensions we usually perceive. In other words, what seems like a mysterious connection to us may make perfect sense when viewed from a fourth or higher spatial dimension, perhaps outside of the time dimension entirely. This is consistent with Richard Feynman's descriptions of electrons outside of spacetime—they can be many things at the same time (superposition) and they can appear to be connected (entanglement) even though they are far apart.

"Walking through walls" using a fourth spatial dimension

It might sound like introducing chaos, to add even one additional spatial dimension, but when you get to know the rules, you can work with it. There are virtual reality and video games that simulate interactions in hyperdimensions. In the video game Miegakure, for example, the player can manipulate a 4D spatial object and it can appear to be a shapeshifter as different parts of it enter the 3D space of the player.[103] To get a sense of this, imagine I place my 3D hand on the 2D world of flatland. If I place my palm down, the residents of flatland would see a roundish shape. As I touch the surface with the tips of two fingers, two round separate dots would appear. They would seem unconnected from that perspective—the residents wouldn't see that both dots are part of one single connected hand. And more is possible: in Miegakure the player's avatar can also appear to walk through walls by slipping into a fourth spatial dimension to go around objects in the 3D world.[104] This is much as the 3D cat (or my 3D hand) could walk over the entire 2D surface of flatland even though 2D creatures would be blocked by nearby objects in their way.

Source: Marc Ten Bosch, https://marctenbosch.com/miegakure/flatland.png https://miegakure.com/

Multiple universes?

According to Michio Kaku, in *Parallel Worlds*,[105] "Parallel Universes, dimensional portals, and higher dimensions, as spectacular as they are, require airtight proof of their existence.... Previously, it seemed hopeless to test many of these predictions, given the primitiveness of our experimental equipment. However, recent advances in computers, lasers, and satellite technology have put many of these theories tantalizingly close to experimental verification."

According to some scientists who study M-theory, a view from the fifth of the eleven dimensions could give us perspective on our own 4D spacetime, much as the 3D cat could see all of the 2D flatland world on this page at the same time. We might be able to see into the future, or see all of space, or a sequence of events over time, simultaneously. The sixth dimension and beyond become even more complicated: Stephen Hawking says they can refer to additional worlds or universes originating from the same initial conditions as ours, and from other initial conditions.[106] The fundamental particles and forces in these universes could have properties different from those we know. From a hyper-dimensional perspective, our universe as we presently know it could also have many possible histories, more like the quantum objects we have talked about. And its future may spread out in an infinite array of possibilities.

Meanwhile, philosophers have pointed to this hyper-dimensional perspective. For example, Jean Gebser, a twentieth century Swiss philosopher, described multiple states of human consciousness, somewhat related to human evolutionary development, that include archaic, magic, mythical, mental, and integral states of consciousness.[107] The first three states of consciousness he called "unperspectival," sharing the characteristic that from these states of consciousness the outside world is generally not seen as separate from ourselves. As humans developed a perpectival approach, for example, as demonstrated in paintings where perspective is portrayed with geometric accuracy, they also developed precise mental capacity for separation and categorization: this not that, here not there. Complex mathematics and technology were developed with the razor precision of the mental structure of consciousness. Looking beyond the mental, Gebser points to the development of an integral consciousness that does not exclude any of the previous, but includes them all in an "aperspectival" view; that is, beyond spacetime. This integral consciousness reminds me of Stephen Hawking's description of a hyper-dimensional cosmos.

Intersection of the finite with the infinite

The gate of heaven is everywhere.

—Thomas Merton

The potential existence of multiple dimensions and the possibility of many worlds invokes something mysterious about our physical being, as humans at the intersection of the infinite, holographic, interconnected reality described by M-theory, with the Newtonian, Cartesian, 4D spacetime that we usually perceive. *It's almost as though we live at the intersection of the infinite, as it interpenetrates with the finite.* I wonder what that might mean for our role at this unique place?

According to many of the great religions, human beings can be seen as conduits between what many would call heaven and earth. But from the point of view of a hyper-dimensional reality, *any so-called heaven and earth would both be tucked into what we are and where we are, right here and now*. And both would be accessible to us right now: we could visualize the worlds accessible to us almost as the infinite jewels of Indra's Net, or even as the hyper-dimensional "gates of heaven" of quantum field theory or M-theory that are tucked into each point in our universe.

"In my Father's house there are many dwelling places. If it were not so, would I have told you that I go to prepare a place for you?" said Jesus, according to John 14:2 (NRSV). As we talk about these other dimensions of M-theory and gates of heaven, this reminds me of descriptions of other realms, including the Kingdom of Heaven. Perhaps these other realms are consistent with physics—who knows? But for humans, living in the world we experience as so finite, this realm would be entered as the mystics tell us: through our inner being, or through the heart. When Jesus says, "I go to prepare a place for you," the Aramaic word used for place, *atar* or *atra*, can literally mean a land or a place, but also a respite or a space for something, or providing an opportunity or giving a chance. He is not necessarily talking about a physical space at all, but a place seen with the heart. This is where we could experience the infinite, connected field within our being. Jesus says, "The kingdom of God is not coming with things that can be observed; nor will they say, 'Look, here it is!' or 'There it is!' For, in fact, the kingdom of God is among you." (Luke 17:20-21, NRSV). The Aramaic word translated here as "among," also translated as "within," for example in the King James Version, comes from the root, *gev*. *Gev* can mean inside, within; or common, held in common, or even in the middle. Jesus could have been referring literally to an indwelling within our physical being (one of the meanings for the Semitic root of this word is "belly"), or perhaps among us, in common among all of us, or even *as* all of us. In a highly interpenetrating reality, all can be true.

In any case, we could say that physics provides a consistent picture of interrelatedness; it proposes a cosmos in agreement with the assertion that we are intimately related with one another and with all reality. And this is consistent with Jesus' insistence that the Kingdom of Heaven is within us. There is no heaven outside of us, or apart from where we are. Any Higher Being in this luminous web wouldn't be outside of us, judging us, but would more likely be right within our own hearts; our own multi-faceted reflecting jewels in the Indra's net of reality.

Questions for reflection:

- What events in your life remind you of the glistening "spider's web" of connection, beyond limitations of time and space?
- What did those moments feel like?

| Chapter 8 |
Why Aren't We Aware of All This Amazing Stuff?
Our Egoic (Spacetime-bound!) Operating System

For now we see only a reflection as in a mirror; then we shall see face to face. Now I know in part; then I shall know fully, even as I am fully known.

—1 Corinthians 13:12 (NIV)

We have the choice of two identities: the eternal mask which seems to be real ... and the hidden, inner person who seems to us to be nothing, but who can give himself eternally to the truth in whom he subsists.

—Thomas Merton, in *New Seeds of Contemplation*

Quantum fields entangled across the universe and the interwoven web of M-theory tell us that things are much more connected than they usually appear. Most people I know have had at least an occasional sense of a connection that extends beyond our logic-based, Newtonian, 4D spacetime world. For example, you may be thinking about a good friend and they call just as you reach out to contact them. Or you may have had an unusual sense of immediacy or intimacy with the world around you, especially when immersed in nature, the arts, or a physical activity requiring your full presence.

But why don't we typically notice our intimate connection within this quantum Field of Being? Of course, we are far larger than the proverbial ant on the garden hose, vast orders of magnitude larger than the quantum world and the dimensions of strings and membranes of M-theory. Our scale of existence is far different from that of the tiny piles of multiple atoms found in two places at once, and is much warmer than liquid helium that spontaneously flows uphill at temperatures just barely warmer than the cold outer universe.[108]

How could these mysterious quantum phenomena possibly apply to us? I don't think anyone has definitive answers to this. As physicist Sean Carroll says, "The fact that we are big, lumbering, macroscopic objects might make classical physics a good approximation to what we are, but our first guess should be that it's really quantum from top to bottom."[109] Austere quantum mechanics, my favorite interpretation, implies that there is only one wave function, encompassing everything: one big umbrella under which all of us, everything, is huddled. The arms of our being extend into the whole universe, in a cosmic inter-play beyond the limits of spacetime, just as the mystics have told us for centuries.

"A finger pointing at the moon is not the moon. The finger is needed to know where to look for the moon, but if you mistake the finger for the moon itself, you will never know the real moon," wrote Buddhist teacher Thich Nhat Hanh. Physics and mysticism appear to be fingers pointing at the same moon: the same relational reality, hidden in plain sight. So, if this highly interwoven cosmic web permeates everything we are made of, why might we miss all of this entirely? The answer may lie in the way we usually interact with the world, in our usual state of consciousness.

Goal-oriented, top-down thinking:
We are way too much in our heads

There is a Zen parable about Nan-in, who was a Zen master.[110] An emi-nent professor traveled to visit Nan-in, climbing a rough mountain-side. He wanted to obtain all of the master's knowledge, confident that he could do it quickly and efficiently. As they sat together, while the professor rattled off all his accomplishments and what he thought about spirituality, Nan-in began to pour some tea for him. He kept pouring until the professor called out for him to stop, shouting that he was filling the cup too full. Nan-in replied that the full cup was like the professor's mind, so full of opinions and thoughts that he would never be able to learn from the master in that state.

The professor sounds familiar. So many of our world's various cultures value learning and doing and accomplishment. The professor's hidden agendas may have driven his desire to quickly acquire the knowledge that Nan-in had (a desire for power and control), and to show how successful he was (a desire for approval and esteem).[111] As a society of achievers, we are used to "making things happen." We generally have high praise for people who have achieved a lot, especially when they have also acquired wealth, fame, and power as a result. Our culture also encourages us to keep our mind busy with thinking, talking, and worrying, often with constant input from media, meetings, entertainment. It is quite full. Overwhelmed by this maelstrom, it is easy to forget who we really are at the core.

And yet, if we practice an embodied, integrated presence we have a chance to respond consciously to anything that comes up, rather than succumb to a knee-jerk reaction that collapses us into emotions such as fear and/or anger, or other reactivity. These reactive emotions can cut us off from our nervous system regulation, and from a sense of presence, and the resources of the wider interbeing—the relational web.

Let's take a look at some of the known ways that we stumble around, seeing only the finger and not the moon. Or, referring to our earlier analogy, seeing only a select small part of the proverbial elephant. For one, our brains filter what we perceive, forming a very specific lens through which we view the world.

We see what we expect to see

"No phenomenon is a real phenomenon until it is an observed phenomenon ... we are participants in bringing into being not only the near and here, but the far away and long ago," wrote physicist John Archibald Wheeler.[112] But cognitive scientists have also shown us that we are participants in our perception of more everyday events, often without noticing at all. Our brains have a preference for seeing things that make sense to us, that fit our model or paradigm of how things work.

In one experiment designed to study this type of preference, people were simultaneously shown two different scenarios, one with the right eye and the other with the left, of one ball encountering another. In one case the first ball (A) hit the second ball (B) and shot it forward, much as would happen with two billiard balls on a pool table. In the second case, ball A passed right through ball B, and in the third case, ball A never touched ball B, but ball A stopped and ball B rolled ahead as though it had been hit (see below).[113]

A

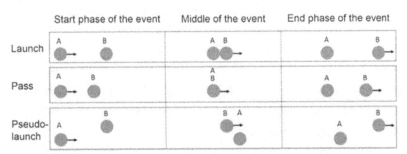

A causal event, such as the "Launch" (top), where one ball knocks the other away, is perceived preferentially to non-causal events, such as the "Pass" event in which ball B doesn't move until ball A completely overlaps it (center), or the "Pseudo-launch" where they miss completely (bottom).
Source: P. Moors, J. Wagemans, L. de-Wit, Peer J (2017): e2932. Licensed under Creative Commons.

Most participants remembered seeing only the first scenario—they didn't notice the others. (This was whether it was shown to either the right or left eye—the experiment was done both ways.) In other words, *we process causal events preferentially*, such as a ball that appears to knock another ball away, as a billiard ball would do. We prefer our familiar, Newtonian world to one with rules that surprise us. *We see what we expect to see.* The preference for perceiving the causal event vs. the non-causal events happens so quickly that it is not a conscious choice: it is made in the brain on a time scale way before cognitive processes can kick in and make a judgment.[114] Our brain makes decisions for us before we even have a chance to decide for ourselves what makes sense!

Inherent bias draws us to prefer our own "tribe."

Inherent bias studies at Harvard have been conducted to assess our unconscious prejudices with regard to various human characteristics such as ethnicity, gender, and religion. These studies show us that our judging minds are constantly making assumptions without our conscious participation,[115] as we subconsciously decide what groups are our tribe. In daily life, these tribes can be in many categories, such as fellow members of a parent-teacher organization, groups of techie entrepreneurs, artsy types, or fans of a particular team (e.g. sports, politics, religion). We often make these alliances to increase chances for our own success, or the success of our families. If we are not conscious of these judgments, they can drive the decisions that form our lives, which use this precious life energy. We can end up seeing just the part of the elephant that we think we need.

We focus on what we need to survive

Our usual perception of the world around us does not reflect the full raw experience of reality. Neuroscientists point to various areas in the brain in which we construct reality, including the formation of our sense of being a separate self, oriented in time and space.[116] As we have seen, time and space may not even be fundamentally real, and are certainly much more fluid and creative than we usually perceive. But our sense of orientation in space and time is crucial to our construction of a practical, evolutionarily expedient model of our own personal role and place in an ongoing complex, and perhaps incomprehensible, reality.

Are we jeopardized if we perceive too much? According to cognitive scientist Donald Hoffman, any conscious organism perceives the world with a narrow focus. We see what we need to see in order to survive, and the way we perceive changes with our situation. Depending on our immediate focus, this can be driven, for example, by our hunger, or our drive to reproduce. Think of a human being out at night looking for food or company, and how the lens they use to view the world might differ from when they are concentrating on their work, for example. Hoffman conducted simulations (called "evolutionary games") and found a shocking result: *in every situation, the various species that saw reality exactly as it was were outcompeted by those who saw just what they needed to in order to survive.*[117]

This could apply to our human ancestors: in order to hunt down prey, we only needed to perceive what was necessary to identify and catch our target. The mental processing required to process all the information possibly available to us (particularly if we used only our head, or intellectual center) would only slow us down, allowing our prey to escape. Likewise, we don't need to perceive millions of pixels to take in a digital image (below). According to this model, our default focus of attention is to select certain aspects of reality, for the most part with a goal to ensure our own personal happiness, such as selecting a successful or desirable mate, having enough food to feed our families, or acquiring social status.

We don't need to perceive millions of pixels (all of the information) in order to appreciate a photo of a cute puppy.
Source: Ildar Sagdejev (Specious), CC BY-SA 4.0 <https://creativecommons.org/licenses/by-sa/4.0>, via Wikimedia Commons

We construct models of the outside world. It is easy to get caught up in our personal reality and view it as the only truth. As a small case, consider frustrating moments in traffic, or when a relationship doesn't go as you hope. You might feel indignation rise up and dominate your awareness as though it were the only reality. How dare they behave like that / have that point of view! Or you might look right past others (drivers of other cars, people in a grocery line) as though they were unimportant, because you don't perceive them as being able to meet a direct need of your own. It's unfortunate, but a common pattern.

I love what physicist Neil deGrasse Tyson says about our egos, and what a different, broader perspective could provide:

> As grown-ups, dare we admit to ourselves that we, too, have a collective immaturity of view? Dare we admit that our thoughts and behaviors spring from a belief that the world revolves around us? Apparently not. Yet evidence abounds. Part the curtains of society's racial, ethnic, religious, national, and cultural conflicts, and you find the human ego turning the knobs and pulling the levers.
>
> Now imagine a world in which everyone, but especially people with power and influence, holds an expanded view of our place in the cosmos. With that perspective, our problems would shrink—or never arise at all—and we could celebrate our earthly differences while shunning the behavior of our predecessors who slaughtered one another because of them.[118]

This would be a world where we are looking after each other, offering each other mercy and lovingkindness.

We see that our brain has a preference for perceiving causal events, and shows unconscious bias and judgments, and makes survival-based choices. Overall, we are paradigm-driven: we formulate beliefs or assumptions about what is important in the world, or models of the way the world works and our role in it, that drive our behavior and even our perception. We might even call this an "operating system."

Seeing the filters we look through: Our egoic operating system

Awakening is an increasing ability to recognize and transcend the
suppositions that frame our basic perceptual field—or in other
words, to be able to look at the filter that heretofore we have only
looked through.

—Beatrice Bruteau[119]

Cynthia Bourgeault coined the term "egoic operating system" to refer to our typical way of perceiving and operating in the world. This is colored by our likes, dislikes, our sense of identification with various groups or ways we prefer to see ourselves, and other unconscious mechanisms.

Our egoic patterns of participating in the world are deeply affected by our formative years, according to Catholic monk, priest, and abbot Thomas Keating. Keating asserted that we have certain needs: for safety and security; affection, esteem and belonging; and power and control. If these needs are not fully met in childhood (and they wouldn't be unless we were raised by unusually enlightened people) they can motivate our actions, as "emotional programs for happiness."

A good indication that the hidden agendas caused by these unconscious emotional programs are being triggered is when reactive emotions such as fear, anger, and pride are stirred up. For example, my emotional program for power and control may give me the hidden agenda or sense of entitlement that I should be able to do what I want, whenever I want. So if I find myself sitting in traffic, I might find myself tensely gripping the wheel, simmering with anger or at least frustrated. I might even start yelling in the car or driving erratically and endangering others, until I catch myself and remind myself to relax. This may sound silly because we know that getting angry at traffic snarls doesn't help anything, but you might recognize some emotional reactivity like this in your own life. Note that in themselves, these emotions are not bad—in their pure forms, experienced by our whole, integrated being, alive in all three centers, they can be useful and help to direct us in action that is beneficial to ourselves and others. It's when they get caught up by our own likes and dislikes, attractions, and aversions that they get more sticky.

The world revolves around us

From the point of view of the egoic operating system (OS), we are the center of the universe: we act in our own self-interests, trying to fulfill our unmet needs for security, affection, and control. This ego-driven motivation is an important foundation for getting along in the world—we form it in order to grow and survive, and continue to use it to operate in the world. But continued pursuit of only self-interest doesn't bring us true happiness or fulfillment—the results are generally unsatisfying. This is a life work for all of us, to see these mechanisms in action, or they can steal away our moments and drive our life direction.

When stuck in our heads or driven by reactive emotions (or the emotional programs for security, esteem, power, and control), we tend to encounter only what we expect, and leave out huge swaths of what we are. We can end up viewing the world around us as something to control or wrestle with, rather than to dance with playfully. In a combative stance, judgmental thoughts, anger, or self-righteousness can arise. As an antidote we might try to push the thoughts or emotions away, to get rid of anything we see as negative. (Just try that and see how long that works!) A common human solution is to project the worst of it onto other people, deciding that they embody all that we wish we were not. This can be the root of various forms of prejudice, or political polarization. The only thing I have found to slowly chip away at this is the contemplative work, and the precious value of working in a group with others who are doing the same type of conscious work, to help each other see all of this in action.

Three-centered balance

Anchored in three-centered awareness (which is somewhat parallel to integrated body-energy-mind, or body-speech-mind in Buddhism), we can see with new eyes, sometimes called "direct perception." Bypassing the dualistic circuits of judgment and categorizing, we can see from a fuller being; from the heart.

Three-centered awareness tells us something different and very counter-cultural: being radically inclusive, it can bring a fuller experience of reality that includes our whole body, mind, and emotions (moving, intellectual, and emotional centers). We become more balanced, and more available to the force of the vibrant, creative, relational field accessible to us at every point in spacetime. The people and the world around us are seen as parts of a whole that includes us, all entangled in the Ground of Being. It becomes easier to step back from the stories of our programs for happiness and view others with compassion, gentleness, forgiveness—in other words, to love others as ourselves.

However, when we are in our heads, or the intellectual center, which dominates in our Western culture, we can be overly focused on thoughts, ideas, images, planning, goals, and lists. It is the Cartesian center of "I think therefore I am." When we are caught up in our heads, there is no one left at the center. We lose access to our full faculties and to our openness to a new way of seeing and being.

In summary, our perception of reality is highly subjective: none of us sees the same absolute reality. Our brains are part of this: they process information selectively to see what we expect to see. We also have unconscious biases and programs running in the background that co-opt our attention, that divert us from participation in the greater whole. And in our usual egoic operating system, motivated by unconscious hidden agendas and steered by our emotional programs for happiness such as security, affection, and control, our actions don't come from true freedom, but from artificial constrictions. Wouldn't it be wonderful to learn to let go of these, to find freedom?

Questions for reflection:

- Are there individuals, or groups people, in some arena of your life (school, work, neighborhood, etc.) that you have tended to judge, or with whom you have experienced "selective seeing," where you saw just what you expected to see? Has this changed over time?

- Look back on one of your recent interactions, perhaps in a meeting with several people or one other person, where you might have felt annoyed, angry, or unhappy. Aside from what the other person or people did, do you think any of your motivations might have been based on a need for control? Or esteem? Or security? Which of these do you tend to manifest?

- Seeing our own emotional programs or disintegrative tendencies is precious, and the seeing comes from a deeper part of our being. Can you view these tendencies with compassion for yourself, and even appreciation for the insights?

Chapter 9

Attuning with the Field that Connects Us
A Unitive Operating System

Petroglyph of person, thought to symbolize Life. (J. Andrews Hayter)

The soul is not ruled by time and space. The soul is infinite. It
blends with the One in infinity.

—Ram Dass

There is a way of perceiving and participating more deeply in the open
field that is always accessible to us. It can be quite counter-intuitive and
counter-cultural, when seen from the hurried, goal-oriented state we so
easily slip into. This more whole-bodied, balanced way of being reflects
an integrated system of body, emotion, and mind, coming together in

the heart. A new operating system is available. I'll take a leap and suggest that from this unitive, or mindful OS we can access an entirely new state of being that recognizes our participation, our interwoven part in the dance of the cosmic web.

We saw earlier that Jesus said the Kingdom of Heaven is within you. He also said "My Kingdom is not of this world" (John 18:36, NIV). Looking at the etymology of the Aramaic word for world, *olma*, we see that it can mean world, but also an age, era, or length of time, or even a state of existence.[120] I wonder if Jesus, speaking on multiple levels at once, was talking about a kingdom outside of time entirely, or perhaps an entire new way of being. Cynthia Bourgeault (and modern mystic Jim Marion) would say that Jesus was talking about an entirely new (and awake!) state of consciousness.[121]

Keep awake!

According to the Wisdom teachings, we would be asleep if we engaged only in one center, for example the intellectual center. This type of lopsided approach affords us only a partial view of reality. And we need more than our Newtonian, 4D-bound points of view and our egoic operating systems to open to the possibilities of an interrelated reality, beyond the limits of spacetime. We just might need an integrated approach, bringing to it more of what we are, that includes all our centers online and a sense of awareness, or presence, that doesn't identify solely with our typical emotional and mental patterns. A more integrated way of seeing, from a greater Whole, brings a new lens to sense the treasures that are hidden in plain sight, and allows us to begin to live in a more expansive way. Visionary Charles Eisenstein points to these timeless treasures, evoking something that sounds like the jewels in Indra's net, or the spider's web after a rain; the mysterious relational field. He wrote: "It isn't that the bull's eye, the destination, home, doesn't exist. It is only that it doesn't exist in linear time. It is like a crystal hanging above our entire timeline, refracting partial images of itself into our world that we recognize as home. That is why the mystics tell us that it is always there, closer than close."[122]

We can get spontaneous hints of this expansiveness as it surrounds us. Something deep within us knows that. It is built into us. And its presence becomes more noticeable as we learn to attune ourselves to perceive and participate in it more fully. Contemplative practices that include meditation, body practices such as tai chi and yoga, and full, integrated immersion in the arts, nature, or physical presence, have the potential to grow in us a new way of seeing and being.

Aided by these practices, we have the potential to see the false self, the egoic OS that we have talked about, and anchor ourselves without judgment in the present moment. It is almost as though we are cultivating a new center of gravity that is not dependent on outer circumstances or even the state we find ourselves in. However, it's important to emphasize that just seeing our false self, or "healing the ego" is not what we mean when talking about a new state of consciousness. When coining the phrase "egoic OS," Cynthia pointed also to an *entirely different way of seeing and operating*: the unitive, or mindful OS.

The contemplative way of seeing and being that synergistically integrates our faculties, our three centers of body, energy/emotion and mind/intellect, is in essence a new operating system for us. And as we'll see shortly, scientists have gathered evidence of a marked difference in our way of perceiving and being as a result of these contemplative practices; evidence of a new OS. But first let's talk more about what this type of seeing might look like.

Turkish Sufi practitioners of whirling, a type of embodied, 3-centered contemplative prayer. (J. Andrews Hayter)

We start with a story on the unlikely topic of root canals, a gritty procedure where the endodontist drills deep into the jaw to remove all of the root beneath a tooth. I had an epiphany during a root canal. I had gone to the dentist for a sore tooth she had been monitoring for a while, and she knew it needed a root canal. She sent me to the endodontist across the way, who had an appointment about half an hour later. So, I went to my car to wait, which is what you do during a pandemic, to limit time spent in the waiting room. As I sat, I had thoughts of dread (no one expects a root canal, or the Spanish inquisition for that matter, according to Monty Python), and noticed that much of my body was clenched: I felt a huge tension in my gut and in my face. But then I thought, gosh, why get all worked up now? You have plenty of time to do that once you are in the chair with their hands and drills shoved in your mouth.

I sat and breathed, feeling my feet on the floor of the car, just present. A chant we had sung for our online meditation that morning came to mind. Based on a poem by Sufi mystic Hafiz, the words are: "And God said, I am made whole by your life. Every soul, every soul, completes me." As I hummed the gentle little tune, it was very calming as the sound resonated in my body. When I went into the building for my procedure I noticed again wanting to panic, but thought, what is really happening now? You are not under threat; you are just standing here in an empty waiting room. I did a little stretching and standing yoga. Then they brought me into the procedure room and numbed my mouth. Again, waiting, I thought, *Here I am in a little room.* Everyone needs to be somewhere. I hummed the tune from the chant. It's odd, but it felt then like sacred space. The room felt filled with a stillness, with gentleness and peace.

The endodontist came in and leaned his head quietly towards me, maybe to listen to the chant. It seemed as though it held a message for both of us. As he and his assistant started the work, drilling away the nerve beneath my tooth, they both seemed almost like columns of light, like holy beings, souls completing God. There were a couple of moments when it hurt and I noticed wanting to close up, to curl in a ball and shut it all off, but instead I thought, it's just a little pain and not that bad. It really wasn't, especially when I kept letting go of the wrenching tension that kept reappearing in my neck, shoulders, and belly in reaction to the loud drilling and jarring vibration in my jaw. I continued to let go of the story of how awful this was supposed to be, to just being with each moment as it actually was. They finally finished, and in the strangest sense I felt as though a gift had been given. Maybe not just to me, but to all of us. I thanked them from my heart, and then drove home. My jaw was over-stretched and my mouth was sore for days, but those moments were somehow holy and life changing for me. And for who knows who else.

I think we are all holy people, doing holy things, all the time. *Whole* people. In the midst of root canals, grocery lines, and bad dreams, I think it's the way we sink into these moments that makes a difference. If we can show up and be present with all our body, mind, and being, these moments can be sanctified. In a way they are always part of an unfractured Whole, but we have the choice: to panic and/or grow grumpy, or to participate in a "divine exchange"—a mutual simultaneous offering and receiving of renewing energy, pretty darned close to what you would call love, or lovingkindness. It is always available, always being offered, and we can accept the invitation to dance with it, or not.

I think you can see a pattern in that tale. I kept getting caught up into a story of what a root canal should be, and noticed my entire body going along with it: tensing, propagating a cascade of neurotransmitters and stress hormones (and starting to cut past the regulating ventral vagal system straight to the fear-driven amygdala). I kept recalling a commitment to see that, to make the counter-cultural gesture of kenosis: letting go again and again to a more relaxed, open space. Being anchored in my body with stretching, yoga, chanting, and basic body awareness helped. I'm not saying that the root canal was fun, or that it didn't hurt. It *did* hurt, but it was just for those few moments at a time rather than a multi-hour story of misery and "poor me." By remaining present to what was actually happening in each moment I had more of a chance to alleviate suffering, both my own and of those working on my tooth. By letting go to a more inwardly free presence, letting go of likes and dislikes, we all had the chance of noticing, together, a more open, generous, and abundant space.

How we see in a non-identified, nondual way:
Moments of Presence

You must live in the present, launch yourself on every wave, find
your eternity in each moment. Fools stand on their island of
opportunities and look toward another land. There is no other
land; there is no other life but this.
—**Henry David Thoreau**, in *Walden*

Presence is an integrated, embodied way of being. We are rooted wholly in the present, noticing our desires and dislikes but not getting caught up in them, or into the stories we often weave about ourselves and our histories. This does not mean that we don't need to address the past: the work we do to see how our past tries to entangle us now, coloring our relationships as we project unresolved trauma onto other people or what we think people think of us, is extremely important. Our past experiences may have shaped what we expect from the world; but we can ground this as best we can, in this body, in this present moment, as it is.

On a more general level we could talk about non-identification. We have so much energy stored up in our stories of who we are: our professions, cultural backgrounds, family roles, voting preferences, and so on. This takes a lot of energy and diverts us away from who and what we really are. As the Sufi poet and mystic Rumi once said, "Your task is not to seek for love, but merely to seek and find all the barriers within yourself that you have built against it." Part of presence and true mindfulness is to learn to see these barriers, and not to judge ourselves for them—that would be just another aversion, another spinning of a story that traps us again. In this type of self-awareness and nonidentification we see and take responsibility for letting go of judgment and all the other self-punitive actions and microaggressions that might otherwise emerge unconsciously from our story of our self, with all of its wants and rejections.

As Cynthia Bourgeault has written: "Every now is a slice of divine being. It is tucked into what we are, and we have access to it." So, what is this "presence"? Is it only for special people, in special moments? We all have our stories, key moments when we have felt particularly alive, sensing an essence of something far greater sparkling through into our present moments. On first look those moments might not seem like the special, desirable ones—they might not be flashy or dramatic. They may seem more like the "in-between," where nothing particularly important seems to be happening.

As a teen, I loved to sing. My mother, a singer in the Metropolitan Opera chorus, taught me a few simple arias. With my naive approach, I would approach the aria with hyper-attention on the high notes (you know, the ones where the divas really shine!). Those notes *became* the aria for me. But as I started to sing, fear would dart into my singing: will I make that high note? Can I open it up and sound like a diva? I worked myself into a state of tension and anxiety, reaching and hoping for moments of perfection. The notes in between were just little stones across a creek, with the great Promised Land on the other side. They didn't really count; there was no glamor in them. In this state of tension my voice would often crack, missing the high note entirely.

One afternoon as I was singing one of those in-between phrases, my mother abruptly stopped me. She explained, dramatically gesturing by extending one arm out from her chest, that *all* of it was the aria; it all had beauty and flowed together. I remember feeling a bit dubious, not really getting what she meant. But I started over, singing the in-between notes with all my heart—and finding melody in them; a coherence and beauty that I hadn't noticed before. This way of singing was much easier than what I had been doing: it felt more relaxed and natural, coming from my chest instead of my throat. What came out of me then began to sound like *music*: connected, flowing, even graceful.

This was a powerful analogy for my approach to my whole life. Most of us tend to gravitate toward the high notes, the sexy "special" experiences. And it is so easy to judge or dismiss so many of our moments, deciding, often unconsciously, whether they are good or bad. We imprison ourselves in a spacetime cage: remembering moments we thought were special, and throwing away precious moments that don't measure up to our expectations or hopes. There is a treasure trove there, waiting for our fully embodied participation.

I'm slowly learning and re-learning that it *all* counts. It is all holy, in its own way. I love the way visionary Bayo Akomolafe describes reality with a wide embrace:

> Once, I lived on the tarred, lonely highways of truth—slugging towards the looming horizons—the promised dwelling places for those who did not waver. The whole world was about being either right or wrong. I was either lost or found. That was many years ago though. Today, when I meet people, I recognize how utterly beyond right and wrong they are—how their lives are symphonies beyond orchestration, how their mistakes and failings are actually cosmic

explorations on a scale grander and of a texture softer than our most dedicated rule-books could possibly account for. You see, something happened on my way—and I lost my coordinates, my map, my directives. Now the whole journey is the destination—and each point, each barren point, just as noble as the final dot. Every splotch of ink is become to me a fresco of wisdom, a beehive of honey, a lovely place— and every aching voice a heavenly choir. The world is no longer desolate and empty and exclusive; she is now a wispy spirit, whose fingers flirt through the wind—a million roads where only one once lay. And I need not be certain about the road travelled—since I arrived the self-same moment I set out.[123]

Akomolafe's talk of the journey being the destination is a hallmark of presence, being *in* life exactly as it is. The state of presence is a type of awareness where we are not pushed around by circumstances or our desires; we are present *in* the experience, anchored in an integrated, embodied way. There is more of us there, to fully participate.

Our integrative moments of presence can be transformative, not just for us but for the world around us; even in the little events of our daily lives. Kabir Helminski says:

Life requires so much of us that none of us can afford to be without our full and flexible attention. More often than we know, moments come that will make a difference in the quality of our lives. These are moments of choice that will never come again. They are moments of service, because others need our presence and attention, and they are moments of understanding in a world of much misunderstanding. But for attention to be fully realized it must be an instrument of presence.[124]

There is so much going on in our world that it can be overwhelming at times, and we may be tempted to give up. But a full-bodied three-centered engagement, practiced in our smallest moments, brings so much more of us to actively engage with the world in a meaningful way. Fully present, we know we are part of a relational reality, a cosmic web of being. And when we engage mindfully, the world is changed, however subtly.

How we recognize and cultivate presence

Attention, taken to its highest degree, is the same thing as prayer. It presupposes faith and love. Absolutely unmixed attention is prayer.

—Simone Weil, in *Gravity and Grace*

Presence is not just an arena for mystics and Wisdom teachers. Presence is available to all of us, and we can cultivate it. One popular movement for cultivating present-moment awareness that people may be familiar with is called mindfulness. In 1979, Jon Kabat-Zinn began working with people in clinics and hospitals, teaching various mindfulness methods such as awareness of breathing, sensations, and gentle yoga postures to bring attention into the body, into the present moment, *without judgment.*

Kabat-Zinn found that these and other mindfulness practices helped people cope with pain and chronic illness. He encouraged people who were suffering to stick with it, to stick with the present. "Keep mindfulness alive even in the darkest moments, reminding yourself that awareness is not part of the darkness or the pain; it holds the pain, and knows it, so it has to be more fundamental, and closer to what is healthy and strong and golden within you," he said.[125]

This can seem counterintuitive: presented with physical or especially emotional pain, I feel a tendency to try to run from it: to distract myself with media, with food, with more stuff, or whatever temporary comforts I can grab onto. Yet this often just temporarily postpones the sense of being alive, with all of its true gifts that are beyond circumstance. Presence is an alternative, countercultural way of being: a way of relating with our fully embodied being anchored in this current moment, not limited by the confines of our filters of perception, or the stories we might tell or believe about ourselves.

The practice of mindfulness can easily be mistaken for an intellectual exercise, such as hyperawareness of each sensation, thought, or emotion. At a retreat someone once leaned over and told me that they felt extremely awkward and self-conscious, sitting at lunch trying to eat "mindfully." I easily make this same mistake, slipping into a frame of mind where I think that mindfulness is some sort of hyper-vigilance of our behavior. But that is all in the head! Presence is far more relaxed, leaning into the wholeness of the present moment, even into what seems unimportant, unappealing or even difficult. Spiritual psychologist Robert Sardello would call it *heartfulness*,[126] rather than mindfulness. More of an inside-out phenomenon, it arises from a different way of seeing, of being, that includes our whole body, our whole being, and a deep acceptance.

This is not the same as blindly accepting all circumstances and giving up our choices. Instead, this kind of ground gives us a strength, a backbone, to act in a way that feels right. As we are immersed more deeply in present-moment experience we have more of us, more resources, to work with. There is no way we could make this happen, but it can emerge in our lives more freely as we practice being willing to show up, to say yes to the present moment exactly as it is. Our true nature is so much more than we usually see, and is in intimate relationship with all around us. We could even call it a new operating system.

There is an alternative to the achievement-oriented, survival-based operating system described earlier, also called our "egoic" (either/or, binary, or dual) operating system, which is sometimes called our false self. We have the potential for a different operating system: that of our true self, our true nature. Called "wisdom mind" by Tibetan Buddhists, Wisdom teachers urge us to learn to function with this non-binary, unitive operating system.[127] With this new OS, we can still see the usual egoic mind in action, but not take it as the only truth, or get carried away with it.

With the unitive OS, more of us (body, energy and mind) is online, meaning that we find ourselves intimately connected to a larger web of Being, or what priest and scientist Teilhard de Chardin called a "relational field." This relational field is said to be our natural home, before our tracks of habit, cultural conditioning and veils of perception cause us to judge, reject, grasp, and look away. Wisdom teachers tell us that it is always present, always giving. It may even be the same field that physics is talking about. As I present more about this unitive, mindful OS, perhaps you can begin to decide for yourself whether these two ways of seeing, of Wisdom and physics, are fingers pointing to the same moon.

The unitive, or mindful operating system, also called seeing with the heart, our integrated organ of spiritual perception, can spontaneously show us another way of being. This alternate way is something like our eyes becoming dark-adapted in a dark room, where we slowly begin to notice things that we could not see previously because our eyes were so used to seeing with more light. Different vision receptors kick in, slowly showing us what is in the room, what was there all along. We start to see a world where meaning, insight, and clarity come together in a new way.

Letting go over and over again, of the binary, judging, enticing thoughts, of ongoing story-dramas, takes courage. Our egoic OS is used to running the show and can't imagine a world in which it is not the boss, taking every chance to judge, to grasp more for itself. I wrestle with this every day! But we can also grow a new muscle for letting go, to a new way of being. In giving up the grasping, obsessive egoic OS we relax into much more of what we are, and in more complete relationship with all around us. It is a type of self-emptying of our full cups that paradoxically opens us to the field of cosmic abundance, of infinite energy and infinite possibility. We could also call it the great cosmic heart: our own heart as part of the infinite interabiding web of Being.

Our holographic participation in the Cosmic Heart

We seem separate, but in our roots we are part of an indivisible
whole, sharing in the same cosmic process. Do we have a con-
sciousness of belonging to the whole and being whole?
—Ilia Delio

I experienced a brief but visceral sense of what I would call a shared, cosmic heart when I was working with a chanting group on retreat. We began by gently sounding "ah" for a while, letting it emerge from our full body as a vibrating channel on the out breath. Not attempting to harmonize, we let our voices and bodies find the pitch they wanted to meet, and varied the pitch slowly and freely to express this embodied, vibrating being.

As harmonies and dissonances merged, our circle started to coalesce. Reminiscent for me of a transition from separate stones to a single fragrance, it felt as though we entrained in a type of quantum coherence, in a unitive field rather than as separate beings. It felt like we were all one being, much larger than my small sense of self. My egoic OS stories, including the litany of inner worries such as "Am I doing this right?", "Is this a good way to spend my time?", "What is going on in the other room where they are doing a different practice?" all fell away. The gathering felt holy, precious, and intimate.

We began to sing Melanie Demore's beautiful song, dedicating it to a group of suffering children separated from their parents: "We are sending you light, to heal you, to hold you ... to hold you in love." I found it difficult to sing at first because I was sobbing, acutely aware that this chant was real, and that our singing made a difference. The energy field in our chant group was real, palpable, and held us in embrace, as one single shared heart. At that moment, I knew in my being that we *are* intimately connected, those of us suffering greatly and those less so, beyond time and distance.

After we all walked upstairs to lunch, I saw several people from my singing group sitting together and felt drawn to them like a magnet.

As I headed over to them, someone else motioned for me to join their table and I didn't want to feel rude, so I did, but felt torn as I sat down, as though I'd been pulled forcibly out of an orbit, as though a part of me had been shorn away. Somehow, mysteriously, our singing group had become a single resonator in a vast field, each vibration synergistically participating in a whole greater than the sum of its parts. Or, a holographic microcosm of a vast shared One, perhaps a Cosmic Heart (I think this is poetically evoked in the photo of the heart nebula).

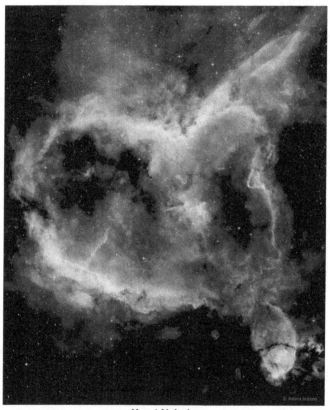

Heart Nebula
Source: https://apod.nasa.gov/apod/ap090214.html

Beyond dualism: Not so limited by 4D spacetime

Our relative condition ... is subject to time and the division of subject from object. That which is beyond time and the limits of dualism is called the "absolute condition," the true state of the body, voice, and mind. To enter into this in experience, however, it is first necessary to understand our relative existence.

—Chogyal Namkhai Norbu

The state of unity of our mindful operating system or attention in the heart can be easy to miss—or our experiences of it can be so brief and fleeting that they don't register with us. But our attention in the heart bypasses certain neurocircuits and learned survival mechanisms. According to Tibetan Buddhist Namkhai Norbu, the unitive OS could be called our "absolute condition"[128] or natural state, beyond time and dualistic subject-object thinking, where we experience a more direct perception from a fully integrated being.

Franciscan priest Richard Rohr reminds us that mystics from all religious traditions gravitate towards daily practices that are receptive to an alternative, more open and unitive consciousness. He calls this *nondual*: in other words, not separated into you and me, right and wrong, here or there, or even particle and wave; beyond the limitation of 4D spacetime. This type of awareness requires self-emptying, much as we saw with Nan-in's cup. Rohr says:

> If we have some good teachers, we will learn to develop a conscious nondual mind, a choiceful contemplation, some spiritual practices or disciplines that can return us to unitive consciousness on an ongoing and daily basis. Whatever practice it is, it must become our "daily bread." That is the consensus of spiritual masters through the ages. The general words for these many forms of practice ("rewiring") are "meditation," "contemplation," and "prayer of quiet," "centering prayer," "chosen solitude," but it is always some form of inner silence, symbolized by the Jewish Sabbath rest. Every world religion—*at the*

mature levels—discovers some forms of practice to free us from our addictive mind, which we take as normal.[129]

Some of the changes that these practices can bring about in our being are detectable in brain scans. As we will see below, scientists have measured evidence of distinct changes in the brain and heart during meditative practices. These results point to the unitive OS as a distinctly different way of perceiving and participating in the world. Functional MRI imaging of experienced meditators has shown their deep reactions to others experiencing strong emotions—evidence that practices such as these bring us into attunement with one another, as members of a wider relational field. To me it is reminiscent of being attuned with the intimately interwoven, hyper-connected quantum field.

The changes in consciousness that occur during moments of presence—either spontaneously or emerging through contemplative practices—point to a different mode of perception and relationship. This different mode can be reflected in our physicality: many scientific studies have shown that regular contemplative practice can cause changes in the brain. Of course, we are much more than our brain—it doesn't tell the whole story. Yet changes in the brain are at least an indicator of a transformation in consciousness, in the quality of presence.

When neurologist Andrew Newberg, MD conducted studies on Buddhist meditators as well as on Catholic nuns who practiced Centering Prayer, he found changes in brain activity in both groups during meditation.[130] Both groups showed decreased activity in the parietal lobe, which is responsible for drawing together our orientation in the world around us and our sense of separation from it. Decreased activity in this lobe is associated with a sense of oneness: sometimes called the Ground of Being, True Self, or Wisdom mind in the case of the Buddhists, and called resting in God in the case of the nuns doing Centering Prayer. Changes in the way the brain works have also been measured in real time during contemplative practices. These studies have shown specific, measurable changes occurring during contemplation.

Our human potential:
Coherent cosmic transmitters of compassion

There is a distinct transition in consciousness that many contemplatives have described as a subjective experience, spontaneously or during contemplative practices. As a scientist, I am reminded of the sudden but dramatic transformation that occurs when a system becomes coherent. As we saw earlier, matter can suddenly transform from a stone-like state to one more like a fragrance, not having to be set in separate "boxes." It begins to behave as a unified whole, a synergetic emergence with distinct "superpower" properties, such as being in two places at once, flowing spontaneously uphill, or being able to levitate a whole train, in the case of superconducting materials.

There is also scientific evidence, detected in the brains of meditators, of a spontaneous process that is reminiscent of a change in state from our usual OS to one of coherence, or resonance. People experiencing this unitive OS embody a deep sense of connection and compassion.

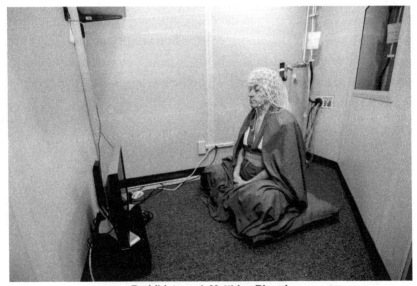

Buddhist monk Matthieu Ricard.
Source: Jeff Miller, Univ. Wisconsin News https://news.wisc.edu/newsphotos/images/
WLBIB_monk_EEG08_2810.jpg

In a collaboration between neuroscientist Richard Davidson[131] and His Holiness the Dalai Lama, researchers studied brain changes in long-time meditators from the Shechen Monastery in Kathmandu, Nepal, and in novices interested in meditation who had been trained for one week. Both groups were instructed to concentrate on emitting a sense of loving compassion during the meditation. The monks had put in at least their 10,000 hours (considered to be the amount of time needed to master something).[132] Their expertise with the practice was such that the researchers thought the measurements were a fluke at first: they asked the first monk to begin and a huge spike appeared in the EEG scan. They thought he must have moved. But as they checked for that, and asked him to turn his intention on and off, alternating for one minute at a time, they saw the spike soar up then drop back down, as the monk performed the practice and stopped.

As the long-time meditators opened to an intention of altruism and universal love, their EEGs showed significant instantaneous increases in gamma brain waves.[133] The gamma waves also became synchronous across the brain ("all one thing"), almost as though the monks had become coherent transmitters of compassion; more like a unified whole. The encircled areas in the figure below (right side) are where the gamma waves increased in the monks' brains, compared with almost no changes in the brains of novice meditators (left side of figure) doing the same practice.

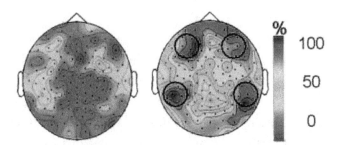

Brain waves in long time meditators doing a compassion meditation showed strong increases in gamma brain waves (right, up to 40 years meditation experience). Few changes were seen in novice meditators (left, trained 1 week only). Electroencephalogram (EEG) electrodes were placed in locations indicated by gray dots, and black circles surround areas with the greatest increases. (Scale bar indicates the percentage of subjects with increased gamma wave intensity.)

From Lutz et al. 2004. Copyright (2004) National Academy of Sciences, U.S.A.[134]

The practice is in the heart

It is important to add that, in this study and others, the monks' hearts showed changes as well, evidence of the heart being entrained with the brain.[135] Some of the first monks in the study had burst out laughing when they saw the experimenters place the electrodes on their heads. When asked why they laughed, they explained that *the practice is in the heart, not the brain!* But because brain changes can be measured with EEGs and imaging techniques, much of the research emphasis has been on these techniques. Again, let's consider these brain changes an *indicator of greater changes in the body / heart / whole being as experienced by meditators in a full-bodied, integrated mind-in-the-heart state of consciousness.* We could say that the mindful OS, in tune with the unified whole, or cosmic heart, includes the physical heart, entrained with the brain and the whole being.

A regular discipline of meditation can also lead to longer-term changes in the brain, not just during the period of meditation practice.

When Davidson's team looked closely at the background gamma wave intensity (before meditation) they noticed it was significantly higher in the monks than in the novices. After peaking during meditation, the monks' gamma waves continued at levels even higher than their baseline after meditation concluded.[136] In other words, the after-effects of meditation form a new baseline for the next session, and are also reflected in lingering traits of compassion in the kind, gentle, patient monks who traveled so far for these studies. Overall health can also be affected: a more recent study from this team showed that when long-term meditators participated in an eight-hour day of meditation, their immune systems experienced immediate positive changes.[137]

Davidson's group found that the longer the monks had been practicing, the higher was the baseline of coherence in the brain. Over time their capabilities built up, much as regular workouts would increase muscle mass. Their longer experience with meditation (and more dramatic brain waves) correlated with a much stronger sense of connection with and compassion for others. This was confirmed in a functional MRI study performed by the same research team that showed the monks' increased empathetic responses to videos of people demonstrating strong positive and negative emotions. Lay people showed much lower responses.

Additional studies of brain changes in long-term meditators have revealed increased activity in the frontal area, associated with emotional regulation and a sense of wellbeing, and in the frontal cortex, associated with decision making and reasoning. Lowered activity is seen in the amygdala, an area in the brain that processes fear and aggression.[138] Changes are also seen in areas associated with greater empathy. These changes indicate physiological evidence of a new basis for behavior, or being.

Overall, changes in the brain during and after meditation point to a distinct change in consciousness that increases over time. Brain changes are reflected in a different kind of seeing, or experiencing the world and our connection to it. This does not imply that any alterations in a felt sense of presence or consciousness are limited to brain changes alone, only that brain changes accompany an overall new way of operating, based less on reactive emotions such as fear, and more on compassion.

However, any Wisdom teacher will tell you that *contemplative practices don't produce anything that was not already there.* As Cynthia Bourgeault has said, contemplation is the fruit of oneness, not the means.[139] Our contemplative practices are more like a participatory celebration, like joining in a dance that is always going on. We can build our capacity for a new OS, and it can change the way we participate in a highly interconnected world.

Blessing an entirely different way of being

Blessed are the poor in spirit, for theirs is the Kingdom of Heaven. Blessed are those who mourn, for they will be comforted. Blessed are the meek, for they will inherit the Earth. Blessed are those who hunger and thirst for righteousness, for they will be filled. Blessed are the merciful, for they will be shown mercy. Blessed are the pure in heart, for they will see God. Blessed are the peacemakers, for they will be called children of God.
—(Matthew 5:3-9, NIV)

When we first look at these beatitudes, or blessings, we see the entirely counter-cultural stance that Jesus takes on the world. He blesses the poor, those who mourn, the meek, those hungering and thirsting for righteousness, the merciful, the pure in heart, and the peacemakers: not the movers and shakers of the world, or those likely to be in dominance. He included everyone, and often ate and talked with people who were typically shunned by society.

A second look, from the point of view of the contemplative stance, tells us Jesus may also be talking about something else: an entirely different way of being—perhaps this new OS we are talking about. Wisdom teachers speak on several levels, and those with the experience and attuned ears (and hearts!) can hear additional messages. (Jesus himself often said "those who have ears to hear, let them hear.")

115

The poor in spirit can also be those practicing *kenosis*: releasing thoughts, preferences, and identifications, much as we do in Centering Prayer and other forms of meditation. This trains a new muscle of letting go when we are out in the world, where we become less likely to grasp or to be reactive: we can see the egoic OS trying to rear up, and make another choice. When we let go of these obstacles the kingdom of heaven, which is always present, becomes more apparent in our lives.

We could also talk about the others, including the meek and the merciful, and the pure in heart, in this other way. The pure in heart recalls the heart of an integrated human being as an organ of spiritual perception: the awakened heart that brings up our inherent faculties, our other ways of seeing and knowing and being in the world. The awakened heart sees from the unity of the cosmic field: our inherent oneness with all beings, and with the Source.

Interestingly, the Semitic root word for righteousness, or *khenuta*, is the triconsonant *kun*. *Kun* can mean to set right or upright, but also to be or exist, to be by nature.[140] In *Strong's Concordance*[141] the meanings include: to be established, stable or steadfast, enduring, or even ready. I hear in this that righteousness could also mean a return to our rightful, whole, original nature. Jesus is encouraging us to open our hearts to find the part of our being that is upright, that endures.

We can learn how to open to this

What would it be like to open and close doors, take some boxes out of the garage, file papers, answer the phone, not as rude interruptions into a carefully sequestered-off contemplative life, but, to the contrary, as living embodiments of the hands-on divinity of daily living?

—Sharon Salzberg, in *Real Happiness*

The intense, coherent brain waves emitted by the dedicated monks, and their highly attuned ability to control and instantaneously transform their focus, is inspiring. Something physiological and very real, beyond our intellectual understanding, is occurring during their compassion meditation practice. And it is trainable—the capacity increases with time spent meditating, independent of the age of the meditator. To me, it points to our human capability for becoming highly compassionate, attuned transmitters of a loving interrelatedness. It gives me hope that we can open ourselves to an alignment with the greater, hyper-intimate and entangled quantum field that physicists also describe. We are not as alone or isolated as it may sometimes appear, and our prayers for others are not just wishful thinking. We *are* connected, as physics implies, and we can cultivate the capacity to feel and act from this connection.

But what if meditation is not your thing? Contemplative practices are a lot broader than just meditation. As an introvert and lover of the arts, I have long wondered about the sense of deep connection beyond time and space that can occur during moments of deep immersion in creative arts, nature, and intimate relationship. These can all be contemplative practices. What can be common to all these things is a sense of presence, as we described earlier. This is somewhat like what we call being "in the zone": being fully immersed in what is here, right now, without reaching into the past or future.

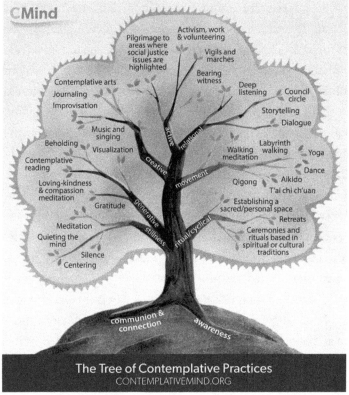

CMind

Activism, work & volunteering

Pilgrimage to areas where social justice issues are highlighted

Vigils and marches

Bearing witness

Contemplative arts

Deep listening

Council circle

Journaling

Improvisation

Storytelling

Dialogue

Music and singing

Beholding

Visualization

Labyrinth walking

Walking meditation

Yoga

Contemplative reading

Dance

Loving-kindness & compassion meditation

Qigong

Aikido

T'ai chi ch'uan

Gratitude

Establishing a sacred/personal space

Meditation

Retreats

Quieting the mind

Ceremonies and rituals based in spiritual or cultural traditions

Silence

Centering

active

relational

creative

movement

generative

stillness

ritual/cyclical

communion & connection

awareness

The Tree of Contemplative Practices
CONTEMPLATIVEMIND.ORG

An array of contemplative practices can train us in new states of consciousness.
Source: The Center for Contemplative Mind in Society (Concept & design by Maia Duerr; illustration by Carrie Bergman). contemplativemind.org.

Contemporary mystic and Wisdom teacher James Finley points to many contemplative practices as paths to cultivate and surrender to the riches of presence, to say yes to the field of Sacred Unity that surrounds us:

A contemplative practice is any act, habitually entered into with your whole heart, as a way of awakening, deepening, and sustaining a contemplative experience of the inherent holiness of the present moment. Your practice might be some form of meditation, such as sitting motionless in silence, attentive and awake to the abyss-like nature of each breath. Your practice might be simple, heartfelt prayer, slowly reading the scriptures, gardening, baking bread, writing or reading poetry, drawing or painting, or perhaps running or taking long, slow walks to no place in particular. Your practice may be to be alone, really alone, without any addictive props and diversions. Or your practice may be that of being with that person in whose presence you are called to a deeper place. The critical factor is not so much what the practice is in its externals as the extent to which the practice incarnates an utterly sincere stance of awakening and surrendering to the Godly nature of the present moment.[142]

Wisdom teacher and activist Barbara Holmes describes a spontaneous, mysterious transformation of consciousness that she witnessed during contemplative singing in a Black American church:

> The worship was inspirational; the singer was extremely skilled. Everyone present enjoyed the music, but there was more. In the midst of worship, an imperceptible shift occurred that moved the worshipping community from intentional liturgical action to transcendent indwelling. There is no way to describe this shift other than to say "something happened." During this sacred time, the perpetual restlessness of the human heart was stilled and transformed into abiding presence. Time shimmered and paused, slowing its relentless pace, and the order of worship no longer took precedence for those enthralled by a joy unspeakable.[143]

The transformation to a timeless abiding presence described by Holmes was not something the group had planned for or tried to make happen. It arose out of a communal intention to surrender, to open to a greater being. The shift she talks about is reminiscent of the coherent shifts seen in the EEG scans of the Buddhist monks, and reminds me again of the shifts in behavior of the physical substances (from stones to fragrances). The sense of timeless intimacy seems consistent to me with the dynamic, holographic reality that transcends spacetime—the cosmic web that connects us all.

Overall, the integrated, whole-being, unitive OS can be cultivated by self-emptying in contemplative practices and can reveal a new way of seeing. Whatever our choices of how to approach contemplation, when we let go of our dependence on the cognitive, judging part of our perceptive process, quieting these areas of the brain and awakening other parts of our being, we can open up to see things as physicists tell us they are: more whole and connected.

How does what we do here change the world?

That is the question that Sister of Mercy Lorita Moffatt asked us on the first day of my spiritual direction training at Mercy Center in Burlingame, California. I was taken aback, surprised—I hadn't really thought of it that way, but it made sense. Contemplative practice is not just for our own personal selves, but in service to something greater. This may not appear to be a huge change, or to be boldly evident in outer acts, but instead it may subtly change the way we interact with the world, in its seen and unseen dimensions. As we cultivate the unitive OS our "baseline for compassion" shifts over time, much as measured in the study of the monks. Its fragrance can waft into life in general, and affect the way we respond in any circumstance. I have a story from one day at work that is not at all dramatic, but is an everyday example of the possibility of opening to something broader, however subtly, even in the midst of very stressful circumstances. An integrated pause can help us respond, not react. As psychiatrist and Holocaust survivor Victor Frankl once said: "Everything can be taken from a man but one thing: the last of the human freedoms—to choose one's attitude in any given set of circumstances, to choose one's own way."[144]

One day when I was working at Stanford's SLAC laboratory, we were engaged with intense focus, preparing to run a complex, costly experiment with a team traveling from Europe. I suddenly heard a very loud beeping alarm indicating trouble—a potential release of flammable gas. The sound rebounded off the concrete walls and pierced my ears and somehow even my eyeballs. My breath froze and choked and I could feel my heart pounding in my chest. I ran over and checked the cabinet and closed off all the gases and vented them safely. But the sound kept crying through the air—a key sensor had been blown. This sensor was essential to doing the experiment safely: we couldn't run without it, and we didn't have a spare part on hand.

I felt the obsessive interior dialogue of an exaggerated emotional center kick in: Oh no, I have failed, I'm wasting time and money, it's going to ruin my life and lose face for the lab, how will I ever outlive the embarrassment. I also felt overloaded, under-rested, and way over-stimulated in the noisy area. I pulled the plug to the alarm to bring the noise down several decibels, and turned away from the people at hand. Nothing I could have said would have been kind at that moment—the sensor was blown because someone new had removed a tank improperly and flooded the chamber and the sensor, so I was also angry. Acting from just my emotional center, without the balance of three-centered awareness, I would have just been reactive. It wouldn't have helped at all.

I tramped up the clanging metal industrial steps to the first door I saw: a single-use toilet. I closed the door and left the light off. With even more quiet, and the intense fluorescent lights out of sight, I began to come into my moving center, my body. Very. Tense. My entire physical being was clenched, participating in a story that I was flawed, I'd failed, I should have been on top of this, on top of (in control of!) every single detail. With a big sigh I breathed deeply, standing in the dark for several minutes. I noted my panicked and angry, frustrated thoughts, but I kept returning to breathing, to my feet rooted on the floor.

I brought attention to my body: clenched fists, hunched shoulders, guts in a knot. Hanging with it, exactly as it was, it felt like I began to slowly fill up the space I was in. I still felt acutely uncomfortable, but a quiet sense emerged that maybe I didn't need to beat myself up. That stance was so counterintuitive: according to the story-making drama-loving part of me, I deserved to suffer, even to brace for punishment of some sort. But as I brought gentle attention to each part of my body, the jagged one-dimensional fragment I had been reduced to, began to fill out and fill up, to be *here*. Various parts began to come back

121

online: my feet on the floor, belly with its tension, chest in constriction, shoulders hunched up in fear, face clenched. As I began to inhabit more of my body, I gradually began to feel more integrated in all three of my centers: body, emotions, and intellect. More present (although still uncomfortable, not "fixed"), I felt more capable of engaging with presence in the situation.

Joy inside the ring that accelerates electrons near the speed of light to generate X-rays at SLAC's synchrotron ring, SSRL. (The beam was off at the time!)
Photo taken by Bert Weckhuysen.

With calm resolve to take on whatever was happening, along with any consequences, I felt ready to respond, mindfully. I walked steadily back down the stairs and carefully reached into the cabinet and unscrewed the tripped sensor. I took it gently into my hand, feeling its cool round metal surface, careful not to touch the sensitive top area. I checked the part number, put it back in and turned on the system again. It had reset (the classic engineer's power cycle trick!) and we could safely run the experiment. Phew! I quickly ordered a replacement part and my colleagues and I proceeded. (I also soon wrote out much clearer, concise instructions on how to use the gas cabinet!)

The moments of embodiment, breathing, and mindfulness in the bathroom helped me to come into a more integrated state. Not forced into just a small imbalanced corner of my being, obsessed with emotional reaction; instead, more of me was present to respond, to work with the situation. It probably didn't look like much from the outside, but I knew the intense storm inside of me that had calmed, helping me to be mindfully present with those around me and with what we needed to do. I could respond from an integrated presence in all three centers, rather than jump into a knee-jerk reaction. For those few moments I could bypass some of my hidden agendas and stories and emotional programs for happiness and be more fully present to the situation, as it was. It also helped me to avoid knocking anyone else into a crumpled-up state of stress, with my own expressions of anger and accusation.

I didn't consciously go up the stairs to try and change anything, but I knew that in my agitated state I had very little to offer. I could have panicked, yelled, shifted the blame, and stayed in an emotional state where it would be difficult to see anything besides my own clenched-up story. But none of us would have gotten very far from there.

No enemy except ourselves

No one is to be called an enemy, all are your benefactors, and no one does you harm. You have no enemy except yourselves.
—St. Francis Of Assisi

Lord, make me an instrument of thy peace. Where there is hatred, let me sow love. Where there is injury, pardon. Where there is doubt, faith. Where there is despair, hope. Where there is darkness, light. And where there is sadness, joy.
—St. Francis Of Assisi

Letting go to a more whole-hearted, full-bodied and integrated state of being, we can become a resource in times of trouble. As Saint Francis urges, we can forgive when we want to hurt, and sow love when we want to hate. And I can add from some of my other life experiences, to

123

bear grief when I want to crumple, and to let go of self-recrimination and learn to accept the infinite relational web that surrounds us and holds us. Our practices that invite the mindful OS help us see a broader picture in which all people are related, suffering together, and are surrounded by and held by a net of Being far larger, more powerful, and vastly more loving than we could ever imagine permeating this mysterious, connected, dynamic, and creative cosmos. Deep inside ourselves we know this as part of who we are, as human beings.

Theoretical physicist Werner Heisenberg once said, "The common division of the world into subject and object, inner world and outer world, body and soul is no longer adequate."[145] In other words, a new, mindful operating system is possible: it is beyond the judging, ego-centered, narrow-minded point of view that is easy to take on while rushing through the world. Our ability to open to this increases as we practice self-emptying and letting go in contemplative practices such as meditation. These practices can alter our relationship with the world, increasing empathy and compassion. Significant changes in the brain and its entrainment with the heart point to a more holistic, synergetic, integrated way of being. These brain changes may be an indicator of a more compassionate presence, where the subjective experience better matches what physicists have told us about the universe: we are connected, not subject to an absolute sense of time and space, and far more multifaceted than we may usually think.

The timeless sense of nonduality, the subjective experience of contemplation described in this chapter, is reminiscent for me of the wondrous Indra's net of the quantum field, of each point or string in space connected to all others. This unified, intimately relational field shimmers inside and outside of us and everyone else, and through this planet, and across the universe. You have likely felt a sense of that connection and affinity at times; this field underlies everything in the cosmos.

No longer limited by separating the world into subject and object, or an inner world and outer world, as quantum physicist Heisenberg says, we could be inspired to take a quantum leap forward, not just personally but as a human race, working together for a common good.

Questions for reflection:

- Have you noticed moments when immersed in the arts or nature or physical activity when your state of consciousness was distinctly different from the usual? What did it feel like?
- What stories do you tell yourself—about yourself, about others, or about your situation? Do you have some favorites? Is there a story you are telling yourself right now that could be opened up, or seen in a new way?
- Have you had an experience of transforming anger and hurt into compassion? How was that physically for you? What internal and or external influences helped you with the transformation?

Chapter 10

No Separation
The Cosmic Web of Life

*A human being is part of the whole, called by us the Universe,
a part limited in time and space. He experiences himself, his
thoughts and feelings, as something separate from the rest—a kind
of optical delusion of his consciousness. This delusion is a kind of
prison for us, restricting us to our personal desires and to affection
for a few persons nearest to us. Our task must be to free ourselves
from this prison by widening our circle of compassion to embrace
all living creatures and the whole of nature in its beauty.*

—Albert Einstein

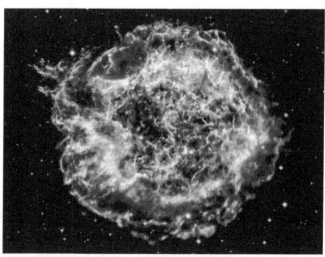

Cassiopeia, a debris cloud from a stellar explosion.
Source: NASA https://apod.nasa.gov/apod/ap210123.html

Each of us has a unique expression of Wholeness: our integrated, present way of being within a larger relational field. As we learn to attune to this field, perhaps through some of the practices mentioned in the previous chapter, or in ways unique to our being, we may be drawn to deepen our participation in it. Anything we do from the core of wholeness propagates the intimate relationality, that we could even call Love, of this field. Our connections hold deeper meaning and are reflected widely in this Love.

My heart is your heart

When I was tiny, at an age when little ones are developing their sense of esteem, of being loved and nourished unconditionally, my parents were preoccupied with my 3-year-old sister, slightly older than I was. She was suffering from leukemia. As she came home for visits, we saw her grow weaker: each time she tried to join me and my older sister playing with dolls we could see her eyes grow more tired and dulled. My mother was gone a lot of the time over the course of my sister's illness, to be at the hospital with her. This illness wore away at all of us, and eventually wrenched our sister from our lives.

My father left us shortly after my sister's death, when I was four. Mother moved with us, her six remaining children, into federally subsidized housing in New York City. In the wake of deep loss and helplessness, she became blanketed in a deep depression. She grew largely unavailable to us, shrouded in work and night performances as a budding opera singer, and eventually in alcohol as well. We wandered our childhood in the worst kind of loneliness, each surrounded by five siblings but feeling zero support. We each coped in our own way.

One day as I was thinking about my father, I could clearly see that I still held him inside me. It almost felt as though I could see his tiny body floating inside the region of my heart. I also saw my anger at him, and the violent arc of my continued rejection of him (even though he left this planet decades ago, a victim of cancer in his late fifties). I also saw that this rejection and anger were taking something from me, leaving me incomplete. I was literally cutting out a dear part of myself, of my own heart.

Around this time, I saw a video of the gentle Buddhist monk Thich Nhat Hanh responding to a boy who asks him, "My father makes me suffer a lot. Should I keep seeing him?" Thay, as his students called him, advised the boy to heal his father in his own heart. He acknowledged that it was difficult, but that he thought the boy could do it because he had been practicing meditation for years. From this inner healing, the boy would know what to do next.

I broke down in tears in front of my computer screen while watching this. Heal, in my *own* heart? This would require a deep acknowledgment of the pain I had been causing myself over these years, of holding onto this resentment. It was so much simpler to blame my father, and to conveniently project my fears and sense of inadequacy in his direction. This pain was my excuse not to look inside and heal, to become whole and live in the world fully responsible for my own life and actions—to more fully express this unique spark of life that flows through my being.

We do this a lot in life: we tend to harbor anger at people who have deeply disappointed or even hurt us; be they family, those we know, or those in power, whose actions have caused us and/or others great pain. But it helps no one. Where do we go with this?

I think the answer is in accessing the great Cosmic Heart. In a connected, creatively vibrant web of a universe, my heart is in yours and yours is in mine. If I can take the anger and resentment inside myself and offer it up, trusting in a greater wholeness, and trust in your wholeness as well, both of us held within this loving field, I am changed and so are you. Like deeply entangled particles, it does not matter how far away, or even whether we are both still alive. We are transformed by love.

We belong to each other. "Nothing exists by itself alone. We all belong to each other; we cannot cut reality into pieces. My happiness is your happiness; my suffering is your suffering. We heal and transform together," taught Thich Nhat Hanh. "When we know ourselves to be connected to all others, acting compassionately is simply the natural thing to do," said Rachel Naomi Remen, M.D. As contemplative practices slowly blossom in our lives it can begin to dawn on us that we aren't just doing this for ourselves, to become more peaceful or less stressed, or even enlightened, whatever that might be. In the middle of pretty ordinary days with their typical ups and downs, we can find moments of feeling connected, almost like superglue, with people around us. For example, one day after I had just returned from a retreat, as I was walking into a store I saw a man near the door asking for money. Normally I would walk by, being brought up in New York City where there were so many street hustlers. But I couldn't walk by this man that day. I tried to step forward into the store, but it's almost as though a magnet pulled me back: to see my brother, my fellow human, to look in his eyes. I gave him some money, as though it were his already. It wasn't mine to give, it was part of an infinite abundance, meant to be shared. And as he smiled a joy leapt in my heart, his delight being mine as well.

As Thich Nhat Hanh said, "If another person is suffering, I am suffering." It makes sense for us to offer compassion, to work toward a common good. It gives life meaning! Sometimes I remember that and embody it, and other times I get lost in the delusions of separateness, seeking what is good for me and my immediate circle or "tribe." In the latter case, no matter how much I acquire or do, I feel a loss, a lack of completion.

In a holographic universe of Oneness, held within a Cosmic Heart, we somehow hold the earth, our planet, and its delicate balances within the palm of our hand. And each of our personal acts in the direction of wholeness makes a huge difference and causes ripples that do change things, no matter how large or full of inertia the current course of events may seem.

Our hearts, as one, may also hold the key to our evolution as the human species. Certainly, the powerful transformative light of our collective heart is needed right now, for our planet and all on it. Mass numbers of species are becoming extinct because of our imbalances. Our own species, too, is enduring a time of dangerous, steep change: we are facing climate change, and our planet is suffering wide ripple effects.

Our societies propagate intense suffering caused by stark inequalities, as we are made blind by our greed, our desire to grow our own tribes at the expense of others. We are also particularly subject to pandemics now, perhaps enabled by our disregard for our planet. Any environmental scientist will tell us that our ecosystems are intimately interrelated. Small changes reverberate throughout food chains and biomes, often in unpredictable ways.

Yet, the effects of small changes can also work in a more life-affirming way. A story I once heard comes to mind, of a drumming circle. In that circle, more like a "U" shape, the leader gave a person on one end a rhythm to play, and then their neighbor picked it up and it propagated around the circle. They were all playing beautifully together! Then the leader quietly, gently gave the person on the opposite end a new rhythm. Gradually, organically, it too propagated and the whole circle morphed into playing the new rhythm, without much conscious effort to change anything.

We can make small intentional changes, for example we can mindfully notice the way we treat people, honoring what Thomas Merton calls "the secret beauty of their hearts."[146] We can pay attention to our use of energy and where it comes from, and to the sources and environmental costs of the food we eat. We can act with careful attention to our purchases with eyes on what has been sacrificed to produce it, and with awareness of our waste stream. We can stand up, in an integrated way, for what we believe in; as Greta Thunberg has done for climate, inspiring many others, and as seventeen-year-old Darnella Frazier did in 2020 by holding firm to make a video of the murder of Black American George Floyd by a police officer. Actions like these come forward as what we must do, not concerned with an eventual outcome, or how many might join us. When we are aligned with the cosmos others will sense it and join in; we can inspire other people, near and far. Sometimes it seems like this is far beyond mere communication: perhaps arising from our deep, timeless connection with one another. This could be how huge movements can start with very small acts, by small groups of people. As Margaret Mead said, "Never doubt that a small group of thoughtful, committed, citizens can change the world. Indeed, it is the only thing that ever has."

What you do matters

You are a precious, shining beam of radiance. By living more into who you really are, you bring new dimensions into any experience. Even the smallest of your actions can be done in a way that either reaches away from oneness, or in a way that embraces it. Any action can become holy, reverberating wholeness throughout the cosmos. The way you pull a dish from the cabinet, present in all three centers, can be in alignment with the heart of the cosmos, affirming and enlivening it. We all move in and out of these moments.

We can also pray for our world, holding it up in our hearts. For me this is the only reasonable alternative to what I sometimes want to do, which is to crumple and sob and lose all motivation, overcome by the magnitude of what we have all been doing to contribute to its current state of imbalance. Father Thomas Hand ("Hando") often told a story of a Japanese man who left his house each morning and rowed across a river, climbed up a hill, and sit there and prayed for the world. In many cultures there are those who believe that this kind of prayer is what keeps our world together. In the context of what we have been learning about the intimate connectedness of our universe, this makes sense.

In a holographic universe, prayer permeates any seeming boundaries of space and time. If I hold someone in prayer, offering our enjoined hearts up to the greater whole, much like the praying monks we saw in the previous chapter, in my heart I know it affects us both in whatever way it is meant to. The scientists saw a unique signal in the monks' brains, that grew stronger with more practice. Something was happening in them, not just the brains, although it's difficult to prove exactly what. Perhaps they were changing the world, however infinitesimally, with lovingkindness.

Cynthia Bourgeault writes of the prayer habits of a dear hermit friend:

Any solitary work of prayer is ultimately communal, and in a powerful though mysterious way it upholds and maintains the life of this planet at an energetic level. Prayer, "piercing prayer"—as Julian of Norwich, another legendary hermit called it—affects something mightily. It pierces to the heart of God, like a strong electric current coursing through the Mercy, subtly rearranging and revivifying everything.[147]

More like love than a puppet-master

This way of prayer is not the same as the new age "you create your own reality," or even the same as invoking a directly interventional God, a puppet-master moving our lives. It is more like a choice, a surrender or self-emptying, to something far greater in this inter-relational web of being. It's closer to "thy will be done," in the sense of claiming our heritage as a ray of this ever-propagating web of being, and stepping forward to embody our unique part in bringing forth a kingdom governed by love. It's almost as though we become a certain shape, a receptacle for a particular kind of energy, shaped by our intention to offer ourselves to the greater field—to the Source of Being. And this is beyond any outcome.

James Finley has said, "If we are absolutely grounded in the absolute love of God that *protects us from nothing even as it sustains us in all things*, then we can face all things with courage and tenderness and touch the hurting places in others and in ourselves with love."[148] Think of the love you may have for a friend or family member. When one of you is going through a hard time, sometimes there is not much to be said or that can even be done (although there are times for doing/helping!). But in certain moments if you just sit there together and be with one another in an open way, it is transformational. The tough things become bearable. This abiding, together, can help bring strength and courage to the depth of our being.

The prayer that radiates through the vast interconnected cosmos is not tied to any specific outcome, and yet in a subtle way it does change things. We realize that awful things can and will happen. Yet, the monks can still offer lovingkindness meditation, awakening a compassionate coherence. And in the midst of pain and suffering we can offer love to one another, trusting that in our hyper-dimensional holographic universe, it has a real effect. We are not alone in any of this.

I got a visceral sense of this once while walking on the Via Francigena—that ancient and medieval road connecting the lands beyond the Alps with the Eternal City of Rome—with my husband. As we arrived into Rome after our long journey, Saint Peter's Basilica was teeming with people. We had come in past the Swiss guards via the sacristy, a large room where everything was prepared for the mass, to get our testimonia after walking our pilgrimage. Past the priests' robes, and all the vessels laid out for the next mass, we slipped down a side hallway to find the "back stage" entrance to the main basilica.

I wove through the crowds in the main church, gravitating to the corner that housed Michelangelo's Pietà. The first time I saw the Pietà was at the World's Fair in New York as a child. I have never forgotten the awe I felt upon first seeing it in the quiet, gently lit room. We filed past on a slow-moving sidewalk, everyone silent, my mother's hand in mine. The poignant picture of mother with grown son laid out in her arms, vulnerable with deep pain and loss, bore into my soul. I may have been especially mesmerized by it because the loss of our sister to leukemia several years before had continued to reverberate in our family, especially in my mother. Grief wafted into our daily moments, even the happier ones, like charred fumes after a devastating fire. Maybe this is what I saw in the Pietà back then: an acknowledgment and even a grace surrounding that pain.

Michelangelo's Pietà, in the Basilica of St. Peter in Rome.
Source: Michelangelo, CC BY-SA 4.0 <https://creativecommons.org/licenses/
by-sa/4.0>, via Wikimedia Commons

On that day at the end of our special pilgrimage, in St. Peter's Basilica, I worked my way gently to the clear partition in front of the statue. There they were! Every fold in her gown, in mother's and son's faces, arms, and muscles, emanated intense emotion and grace. As I gazed at the Pietà I was struck by the piercing, wrenching loss of what seems to us the ultimate separation, death. Yet I know it is not the end of that story, nor of any of ours. Mary's left hand reaching out, aimed up to the heavens in a gesture of loving surrender, reminds us that much more is going on.

Tears poured out of me, a spontaneous emission of all the tension roiling through me over the past couple of weeks. On the Francigena, in addition to all the wonderful things I had seen and generous locals I had met, I had also encountered my own selfishness. Walking unconsciously, I might not notice someone walking past and wouldn't make way for them. Or I might assume it was my husband's job to take care of many of the little things we needed to do to get through the day, such as calling ahead to make sleeping arrangements. It felt humbling and awful to see these traits in myself, but so crucial. As I cried and apologized, my husband gently said, "We all learn a lot about ourselves on these walks."

Leaving the Pietà, I wended through the crowds in St. Peter's. Seeking a way to be with the thick, oozing sensation vibrating in my chest, I edged around to the Blessed Sacrament Chapel. It was protected by red ropes and signs making it clear it was not for tourists: this place was not for gawking. I told the guards, *"Vorrei prighere,"* I would like to pray, and they let me in. Not wanting to disturb anyone, and even wondering if I really belonged there, I sat down as gently as I could on a bench near the back. Quickly, I felt transformed: something a lot larger than any of us was going on. My skin tingled and I straightened up on the bench, drawn into this larger field of Presence. I could almost taste the energy in the room, and the wispy fragrance of centuries of sincere prayer.

A few rows ahead of me a young man with blond dreadlocks and a woman in colorful woven clothing held each other closely and lovingly, seeming to bolster one another in some deep shared trial, perhaps sorrow at a loss. Shrouded in stillness, priests and nuns around the room bowed their heads: not offering solace to others for now, but earnestly expressing tender devotion, seeking meaning and guidance from the raw depths of their own being. Everyone in the room seemed to be on their knees, including myself, at least in our hearts if not on the kneelers in front of the seats. Humbly and deeply seeking the Real, beyond all thoughts and desires: the Real beyond time, and beyond our many faults and limitations.

Quieted in body and soul, I felt as though the arms of a deep prayer, one that had been there for ages, came and enveloped me like a warm and gentle blanket. Touched by the embrace, tears overflowed from the quivering pool in my chest. I heard a gentle voice from inside lovingly say, *Why are you crying? I'm right here.* The tenderness of it, the presence, seemed to awaken me, to open me. I looked up, scanning the room for its source, thinking. *Really? You are really here?* And yet knowing without a doubt that it was true, my heart opened in love, in gratitude.

I made the connection later that the chapel in St. Peter's was the room where the Corpus Christi is on display, the bread that many believe has been transfigured/transformed into the Body of Christ. Others think of it more as something unfathomable and unknown. Yet I got the feeling that the unknown longs to be known. It was reaching for all of us that day. And all days. And if we feel called to say there is a Higher Being, that Being is closer than your own skin, your own heart. The voice may be subtle—it is in quiet that we are likely to hear it. In most of my ordinary moments of grumpiness, selfishness, or judgment, I may be too preoccupied to notice something like this. Or, I might have just assumed this was my own emotional imagination (perhaps it was!). But I encourage you to listen to the quiet voice of encouragement, affirmation, and love, within *you*.

Seek and you will find

> *Ask and it will be given to you; seek and you will find; knock and the door will be opened to you. For everyone who asks receives; the one who seeks finds; and to the one who knocks, the door will be opened.*
>
> **—Matthew 7:7-8 (NIV)**

If hearing a quiet voice within sounds difficult, or not related to your life, in almost all of the major spiritual traditions one crucial factor is persistence. We are all human with our myriad mistakes and issues, but when we ask, when we step forward, a loving universe responds to us, coming to meet and assist us in our journey, whether in life or in our journey beyond it. Lewis Keizer translates the Greek present imperative for the verse above in Matthew 7:7 as: "Persist in asking, and it is given to you; persist in seeking, and you find; persist in knocking, and it is open to you."[149] Whatever your journey, if you are seeking deeper meaning, especially in such a roiled world, keep asking, keep seeking, keep knocking and you will find what you truly need. The loving quality of the cosmos is always on offer, and some mystics even say that your seeking is actually the Wholeness seeking *you.*

This love is beyond death, as well. I think many of us have sensed at least momentary wafts of a presence, an intimacy with someone who has passed through the door of death, even as we feel the grief of loss. Many claim that death is just a transition to another side. At one point Father Thomas Keating even called it, with a twinkle in his eye, a "promotion." He said: "Death could be looked upon as the birth canal into eternal life. A little confining and scary, maybe, yet it's the passage into a vastly fuller life. Eternal life means perfect happiness without space or time limitations. It is spaciousness itself. You begin to taste it in deep contemplative prayer. You realize that you don't give it to yourself; it's already within you."[150]

A few years ago, a young, gifted friend of mine was passing away, succumbing to cancer. When I got to his room he was in the throes of his final belabored breathing and was on oxygen. His parents and a friend and I prayed, assuring him, "You are not alone here, and you are not alone where you are going. You are loved here, and you are loved where you are going." As I sat in meditation while his parents tenderly spoke with him, I began to notice a feeling of light, peace, and presence in the room. It seemed as though a hole had appeared in the ceiling, soft around the edges. Two beings were up there at the edges of the hole, gently waiting there to welcome him. Surely, I couldn't have seen them with my physical eyes, but somehow I saw them clearly: I knew they were there. While we held and prayed with Michael, I saw his presence join them up there. There was a sense of wholeness, peace, light, love, and even joy. He looked back down, radiant, and it felt as though he were saying, "I am fine. I am whole. Please let them know."

In the midst of terrible circumstances, the glue that holds all of this together is love. It's the only thing that makes it bearable. As he grew more ill, Michael's circle of friends banded together and collectively let him know that he was not alone, he was cared for, and that he was loved. People reached out and helped by giving him rides, taking him to dinner, or by including him in trips to the park, the movies, and other things he treasured. Two months before he died, over the red-checked tablecloths in one of his favorite Italian restaurants Michael sadly told me that his doctor had recommended hospice. I said, "I'm so sorry," and sat with him quietly for a minute. Then I asked him if he would like to pray, and he nodded. When I asked what he would like to pray for, he said "For hope."

In some way, his prayer was answered, although unfortunately not in the way he would have preferred. It was manifested in the hope that we would care for him, and for each other, through his illness and passing. Also, in the hope beyond all circumstances: that Love is with each and every one of us, and that we can sometimes sense the fragrance of this love and light, and pure eternal health whatever we are going through, and when we leave this earth. The day after Michael died, I was feeling the grief of loss and pondering all of this and what it could possibly mean. I was drawn to walk downtown, and while passing by a local bookstore I picked up a book from a sale shelf outside, called *Living Consciously, Dying Gracefully.* It fell open in my hand to a page with a description of someone passing away. One of the authors, Becky Bohan, saw a portal in the ceiling open, with loving beings on the other side, much as I had experienced the day before.[151] My heart dropped open as I read this, and my skin tingled as it often does when confronted with something much larger than myself. I bought the book and curled up right away on a soft cushion near the front window of the bookstore and opened my laptop, urged to begin describing the amazing process I had witnessed of Michael's passing to the next place. I had felt unsure about sharing my experience and wondered if I had imagined the whole thing. But on reading that, especially as it fell open into my hands the day after he died, it felt like confirmation. *"Please let them know."* Yes, none of us is alone here, even if we think so.

Encouragement and the eyes of the heart

I also wonder, why did I see those beings in the portal above Michael that day? Why did Becky Bohan see them, and why was she drawn to write about it? I don't know. It seems that the validation I got from reading her story was encouragement to tell my story, to give hope and encouragement to you. Maybe you have your own stories to tell, too.

I also wonder about the connection of seeing those beings that were in the portal in the ceiling, to the potential existence of other realms, in the context of a hyper-dimensional universe. These realms would not be seen with our physical eyes and ears. Like the slit experiment detectors rooted in this 4D spacetime, our physical senses detect objects within three-dimensional space, played out in time. But with other lenses outside of spacetime, the eyes of the heart, these realms become more accessible. As Saint Exupéry said in *The Little Prince*, "And now here is my secret, a very simple secret: It is only with the heart that one can see rightly; what is essential is invisible to the eye." When I read that book to my children when they were young, my son asked me what it meant. As a budding meditator at the time, I assured him that the heart connected us with so much more than we could see, and that the connection was very real. The contemplative practices I was learning taught this, and the experience was palpable—we *are* connected, beyond 4D spacetime.

Cynthia Bourgeault calls the realm closest to us, perhaps also called the Kingdom of Heaven, the imaginal realm. This term is not the same as imaginary. She says, of the imaginal realm:

> The imaginal realm is *collective and evolutionary*; its ultimate purpose is to guide, shape, nourish, and, where necessary, offer course corrections to our entire planetary and interplanetary unfolding. As an objectively verifiable realm interpenetrating our earth plane and operating at a twice-higher frequency of spiritual intensity and coherence, it is a life within a life, and its laws, interpenetrating our own,

provide the inner template by which the outer unfolding can proceed rightly.

Therefore, it is also and primarily supremely the realm of *cosmic assistance*. It is the "place" from which saints, teachers, masters, and all manner of abler souls reach out across the apparent divide between the worlds to support or where necessary modify earthly outcomes in tandem with willing and attuned hearts here below.[152]

Willing and attuned hearts—these can be ours! We are not alone, we are partnered by realms of wholeness and support present with us, right here and now. This world—the visible and Newtonian as well as the invisible and hyper-relational—points to a vast, even playful signature of a loving, creative universe. And the confluence of the visible and invisible, the possibility of infinity and wholeness, lies within and around us. Where else would it be, in a highly relational, interwoven cosmic web? And this connection is not created by anything we do, and cannot be broken.

This unbreakable wholeness shows up in physics, too.

We can't break the connection

In a recent quantum computing experiment scientists discovered that entangled quantum states are surprisingly robust, resisting disturbance. In a way it's like a holographic memory—if part of it is lost, all the other parts of the hologram, however widely scattered, hold the information and its integrity is sustained, impervious to loss or disturbance. In the simulation experiment, physicists took an entangled state and collapsed it into separate states by making a measurement. When we previously saw the slit experiment the measurement process seemed like it meant the end—the poor little particle smashed against the detector appeared to have lost all its freedom forever. But this more recent experiment points to something else: when the physicists did the equivalent of *marching the quantum system back in time*, they were surprised. The system fully recovered its entanglement, showing that its coherence lay out side of time, and outside of attempts to damage it.[153] I found that study inspiring, a beautiful demonstration of quantum states being outside of spacetime limitations. In this scenario, Schrödinger's cat is revived to its nondual state, outside of time.

I am tempted to relate this back to a Wisdom point of view: even if we do behave poorly and make misguided actions based on our incomplete or biased views, there is a thread, a coherence that continues, that has always been there. What is important is not lost: the infinite creative quantum field of love bears all things.

I'm reminded of a scene near the end of the 1972 production of *Jesus Christ Superstar*. It's an old production but so creatively done that its timeless quality hits home in my heart every time. After the Passion story of Jesus' betrayal and trial has played out in the Israeli desert, all the actors climb back onto the production bus to head home. The actors who played those whose blind actions led to Jesus' death, including Herod, Judas, and Pontius Pilate, enter the same bus door as those who played Jesus and his disciples, including Mary Magdalene and Peter. All the actors are kind to each other, making way for each other to climb the steps into the bus. The story, the drama, has been let go and all is well, all is forgiven. The wholeness has always been true, throughout the entire story that plays out.

In the midst of our suffering, the cosmic heart penetrates every single moment, every heart. It's ours to learn to listen for the small voice, to commit to cultivating a clear heart, our organ of spiritual perception. By way of the contemplative practices, we can discover freedom and a new way of seeing and being in the world. Free from the agendas of the egoic OS that are driven by the programs for happiness, in this state of being we find that all is well, all is forgiven, all is held in love.

Here all the time, a treasure worth finding

*Understanding science doesn't make God smaller. It allows us to
see [God's] creative activity in more detail.*
**—Russell Cowburn, Professor of Theoretical Physics,
Cambridge**

Whether you call it Sacred Unity, God, Universe, Ground of Being, the Source, or One, it is not out there somewhere, but is written into what we are and where we are. The Aramaic word that Jesus used, often translated as "heaven" (as in "Our father in heaven," or "Blessed are the poor in spirit, for theirs is the kingdom of heaven") is *shmaya*.[154] From Aramaic, a language in which words have multiple meanings and individual syllables have deep symbolism, almost as invocations, mystic Neil Douglas-Klotz poetically interpreted it to mean "a sacred vibration that vibrates without limit through the entire manifested cosmos."[155] The heaven that shines throughout all creation is beyond 4D spacetime; we have access to it at any point in space or time. As Thomas Merton said, "The gate of heaven is everywhere."[156]

We can awaken to be more aware of this liminal space: the invitation to expand our awareness is always being offered. There are some times when we can hear the echoes of an interwoven luminous realm better than others. The more we practice self-emptying and listening, the more we will hear it. Sometimes the sense is subtle: we can easily overwhelm it with our own hyperfocus or grasping, based on our egoic OS, likely seated in just one of the three centers; intellectual, emotional, or physical. But I do think the invitation is being offered all the time. Where could the Source of this loving, relational reality, the luminous web connecting all beings, ever *not* be?

When we discover and live from the coherence in our being, we discover that we are in a relational field with all beings, with a mystical spark at the center that connects us all. Merton saw this clearly at the corner of fourth and Walnut, and Teilhard de Chardin saw this and his writings are permeated with it. In *Cosmic Life*, he said, "To live the cosmic life is to live dominated by the consciousness that one is an atom in the body of the mystical and cosmic Christ. The man who so lives dismisses as irrelevant the host of preoccupations that absorb the interest of other men: his life is projected further, and his heart more widely receptive."

Much as the sea pickle that we saw earlier, where an agglomeration of many separate organisms worked together to offer new properties and capabilities in an exchange between the individual and the whole, Teilhard envisioned our human destiny to come together in a way that the whole is greater than the sum of its parts—as part of a dynamic cosmos evolving toward, and guided by, an Omega point. The Omega point, much as the singularity that presumably preceded the Big Bang, would be outside of time entirely. Teilhard asserts that from timeless time, it would be providing a template guiding the long arc of evolution, to a reunion of that which was never separate in the first place. For him this driving force was Love itself, the cosmic Christ that is also outside of time. This is beyond the specific incarnation of Jesus even; the Word that brought all into being from the very beginning (paraphrasing the opening of the Gospel of John). As Richard Rohr said, "Christ is not Jesus' last name, but the title of his historical and cosmic purpose. Jesus presents himself as the 'Anointed' or Christened One who was human and divine united in one human body—as our model and exemplar."[157]

Teilhard related the Omega point with the Body of Christ; of all humans working together as individuals but in sync, as part of the great cosmic heart. The words from St. Paul's first letter to the Corinthians may then take on a different hue, read from this greater cosmic context:

> For just as the body is one and has many members, and all the members of the body, though many, are one body, so it is with Christ. For in the one Spirit we were all baptized into one body—Jews or Greeks, slaves or free—and we were all made to drink of one Spirit. Indeed, the body does not consist of one member but of many.... As it is, there are many members, yet one body. The eye cannot say to the hand, "I have no need of you," nor again the head to the feet, "I have no

need of you." On the contrary, the members of the body that seem to be weaker are indispensable, and those members of the body that we think less honorable we clothe with greater honor, and our less respectable members are treated with greater respect; whereas our more respectable members do not need this. But God has so arranged the body, giving the greater honor to the inferior member, that there may be no dissension within the body, but the members may have the same care for one another. If one member suffers, all suffer together with it; if one member is honored, all rejoice together with it. Now you are the body of Christ and individually members of it.[158]

Just as all began (from the Big Bang, or the Word, depending on whether you are talking about physics or the New Testament) and expanded into the myriad forms that are permeated with the One, all returns to Oneness, which could be described as the cosmic Body of Christ. This is echoed in the Gospel of Thomas where Jesus says, "I am the light shining on all things. I am the sum of everything, for everything has come forth from me, and towards me everything unfolds. Split a piece of wood, and there I am. Pick up a stone and you will find me there."[159]

The mystical Body of Christ: Abide in my love

As the Father has loved me, so I have loved you.
Abide in my love. —**John 15:9 (NRSV)**

When I read the phrase, "As the Father has Loved me" in Aramaic, the word used for love is so completely unconditional, not dependent on anything we might do to try to earn it. The root also means to *kindle* (the same root is used in Luke 12:49 (NRSV): "I came to bring fire to the earth, and how I wish it were already kindled"). It also means to *incite* to love. This invokes a very active, vibrant love: the human desire for Wholeness, for the Source, is inspired by the desire of the One for us. This Source, this Oneness has loved us, flourished us, and blown on us, like kindling a fire. Then Jesus says, "so I have loved you": he too has blown, kindled this love in humans.

If you feel open to it, take a moment in your body, your being, to notice your breath. Imagine receiving a vast lovingkindness as you breathe in, and blowing, kindling within every cell of your body, as you breathe out. As you do this two or three times, where do you feel this kindling most in your being? Some feel it as a warmth in the chest, others have described it as a glow over their skin, or tingling within the limbs. If you don't feel anything, see if you can connect with your *desire* to feel it: this too is real.

Jesus then says, "Abide in my love." That can be seen as the practice of Centering Prayer, or other contemplative practice—whether it be a form of sitting meditation, or a daily prayer practice that can be done walking about in the day or sleeping at night, we are invited to abide, or rest deeply, in Love. The word "abide" in Aramaic, *qevah*, can also mean to wait, hope for, or expect, and even to continue, to endure. But in typical Aramaic fashion where multiple levels of meaning can be found in one word or phrase, it also means to collect, to bind together. This collection can be done in our own being, binding together as an integrated person, to use Teilhard's word. Alive in all three centers and willing to remain present within, bearing with whatever state we find ourselves in, with whatever is before us, fully present in an embodied way. This affects the whole, as we continue, endure, as one coherent diamond jewel in the integrated net of the cosmos, reflecting all other jewels. That is part of the practice of abiding: as this integrated being we open up, let go to the greater Whole, radiating the fruits of the spirit, as nourishing food for the cosmos. The connection begins within our integrated, collected being, and extends to coming together in a single Wholeness: still unique, yet gathered as One.

In the Aramaic Peshitta New Testament the word that is often translated as love in "Abide in my love" is one we have seen before, *rachma*. This is the mercy that surrounds, nurtures, encompasses. The Semitic root for this word is "womb," like a mother loving completely and encompassingly. So, we are invited to abide, endure, collect together in that generative compassion. Abide in my love, my mercy, my encompassing compassion; love one another.

The Web starts with coherence within

So how would people even begin to come together in a synergetic way that requires each one of us and the talents we have been given, to jump in the game together and invest these in a way that brings forth a treasure we could not even imagine? It is not going to come from our egoic beings with all of our personal agendas—it can only emerge as we learn to let go and hold true to the wholeness within each of us, the thriving life force that pulses uniquely through the prism of each being. As each of us learns to dwell, to abide, within our integrated, complete being, that coalesces in a greater whole—because it recognizes its original nature as never having been separate at all, as part of the fabric of the comic web.

Earlier when we discussed coherence in physics, we saw that it could lift an entire train. We also saw that in a hologram, the more pieces we have the better resolution we get of the entire picture. As we become more coherent within our own being and learn to let go of our usual operating system to an entirely different way of seeing and being, the more we can sense the Whole that we arise from, that we are inherently part of, and that Teilhard says we are evolving towards. We can act from that.

Recalling the monks whose brains were in a coherent state as they sent out compassion, imagine what could be, if together we practiced and grew the muscle of sending out compassion and other fruits of the spirit. This could change our physicality as it did theirs and, in the highly interconnected cosmic web that permeates the universe, would change the world. We wouldn't even need to know where it was headed (in fact, its true nature lies outside of 4D spacetime) but we could just join in, aligning with the living, dynamic flow of exchange of the cosmic web that we see laid out by mystics and physicists.

Spirituality in alignment with science

Science, in all probability, will be progressively more impregnated by mysticism (not in order to be directed, but in order to be animated, by it).
—**Pierre Teilhard de Chardin**[160]

Overall, with this interweaving of science and Wisdom, I hope you can see that a reasonable spirituality *can* be in alignment with science. We are encouraged to look again, to trust our desire and hope for deeper connections, beyond a set of "beliefs." We can cultivate a spirituality consistent with science, not in conflict with it. In a holographic universe, where every single point contains all others, there would be no Grand Being *out there*, separate from us. We know we don't stand hapless while some old guy in the sky judges us, ready to start randomly smiting like Thanos in the Avengers if we don't measure up. A lot of religious education is still stuck in this dualistic cosmology, or the Newtonian concept of separate, solid objects interacting. It's hard to take anything seriously if it's based on those old, limited paradigms.

I love the picture that modern physics presents instead: a single whole, each point intimately connected with all others via interwoven hyper-dimensional fields. In this unified, relational field the One, Wholeness, is here in each of our hearts, right now.

And, as Teilhard points out above, the alignment works the other way as well, as mysticism helps us to *animate* science in a way that helps us better relate its significance to our own lives. Science aligned with mysticism can also begin to make more sense; and it can have more meaning for us as part of something far larger than we can fathom.

Physicists and mystics: Pointing to the same thing?

Throughout many millennia, mystics have experienced and written about a wider field of relationality; a Ground of Being underlying our existence. Physicists are just now seeing a world that is far more consistent with this wider, luminous, interwoven reality. Physics showed us that the vacuum, what we call emptiness, is not empty at all, but is teeming with creative potential and abundance. We've seen that atoms contain mainly empty but force-filled space, and universe-sized fertile fields abundant with infinite energy bear forth particles or give them mass. The interwoven, entangled hyper-dimensionality of these fields points to a holographic web of interplay and interpenetration, permeating what we are and where we are: an infinite, creative and fertile connectedness, a cosmic web of being. What a beautiful message to find embedded in our universe!

Mystics and scientists are pointing to the same thing: fingers pointing at the same moon. We don't know in the intellectual sense, and we can't really measure it. Physics is governed mainly by mathematical equations, but humans have other faculties and an inherited, natural access to the liminal space integrating the material and immaterial. It's up to us, guided by the Wisdom teachers, mystics, and poets, to *embody* the musical score of the mathematics of modern physics. As Einstein told us: we don't want to perceive Beethoven's symphonies or the mysteries of the cosmos in terms of wave pressure or mere mathematical equations—we want to play it out, to hear the music. And we may want to join in and sing, even dance, with our fully integrated being.

We are made for this! We sense our participation in the cosmic shared heart when our seat of consciousness is in the heart. With this new lens, a new way of seeing, an integrated awareness can emerge spontaneously. When walking in nature, immersed in the arts, at the communion table, or even hanging on the edge of life at a birth or death, it can loom in and take over, showing us the way. We can cultivate our intention to make room for the cosmic shared heart within the luminous field of being, by practices where we explicitly break our habits of rushing, running frantically, grabbing onto the next thought, imagining the future, or ruminating on the past, positive or negative. We don't participate in the sense of doing something, as we might usually conceive it, but as letting go, relaxing into the pulsing flow of its constant pregnant, inter-abiding invitation.

Our world is depending on it.

- You are invited to consider what has been presented here, the mind-opening approaches of mystics and scientists, and ponder how parts of it may have touched you. If some of it rings true, what might it mean, for you?
- How might these lenses be applied in your own life? In this very moment? Blessings on your journey.

Acknowledgments and Permissions

In deep gratitude to the scientists, mystics and Wisdom teachers through the ages, who have always been pointing fingers at this beautiful moon.

Wisdom sisters: Thank you for the many conversations, and for listening when I started ranting about physics, encouraging me and yet grounding me in a real-world, present, three-centered awareness. Thank you Faye Cox, for bringing Cynthia and me together on your related project for Hourbooks. I look forward to its fruition.

Janet: Thank you for the encouragement, the gentle wise guidance. Some days when I wanted to give up your words brought new life into this, helping to shape it into something that could better bridge worlds, not just between science and spirituality but between a complete nerd and the rest of the world out there. A lifeline, in a way. Also for encouraging me to be authentic, to find and express my own unique voice.

Thank you to dear ones (Judy, Heather, Catherine, Paul) who were willing to read early versions of this and provide kind, loving advice, encouragement, and even proofreading!

Cynthia: So much of what you have written and said is interwoven into this book. I love the way you open up the universe!

Steven: Thank you so much for teaching me, for helping me to discover more of what we are and where we are, for pointing to this incredibly radiant reality that shines though all our moments exactly as they are.

Thank you to my main scientific mentors: Kevin Cadogan, Leroy Chauffe, Kenneth Sauer, Piero Pianetta, and Bert Weckhuysen.

Martha: Thank you for helping me to add kindness, love, forgiveness, and joy to the mix, in your open-hearted embrace of God within me and within all.

Kathleen: Thank you for encouraging me to listen to the teachers within.

Bob Stahl: Thank you for bringing mindfulness alive for me, filled with lovingkindness.

Thank you to family: To Paul who has always supported and encouraged me, and loved me unfailingly through the scary moments. Your kind heart shows through! To Janine and Max, and to Ever, for the joy you bring to life and the warmth and all the kindness. You are really good people! And Max, thank you for your openness to this odd project of mine, and to your artistic rendition of a Calabi-Yau space, bringing out its music and beauty.

For permission to quote from Daniel Ladinsky poems: "HeAsked For Charity," "Spiritual Health," and excerpts from "No One Will Begrudge Me" and "He Desired Me So I Came Close" are all from the Penguin book, *Love Poems From God: Twelve Sacred Voices from the East and West*, by Daniel Ladinsky, © 2002 and used with permission, www.danielladinsky.com. The excerpt from "Forgive the Dream" is from the Penguin book, *The Gift: Poems* by Hafiz, by Daniel Ladinsky, © 1999 and used with permission, www.danielladinsky.com.

Thank you so much to the talented staff at Monkfish: Paul Cohen, for believing in me; and Anne McGrath, Jon Sweeney, and Colin Rolfe for all your help.

Thank you to Mystery, leading me from the very start of this, drawing out words and personal expressions of the awkward places in me where your infinity meets my apparent limitations. Thank you for your patience, your guidance, and your insistence on loving us exactly as we are, and for beckoning us to the Wholeness we never left.

Resources for the Reader

If you want to read more about the physics, try these books:

- Sean Carroll, *Something Deeply Hidden: Quantum Worlds and the Emergence of Spacetime*. (New York: Dutton, 2019).
- Sean Carroll, *The Biggest Ideas in the Universe* (New York: Dutton, 2022).
- Neil deGrasse Tyson, *Astrophysics for People in a Hurry* (New York: W.W. Norton, 2017).
- Brian Greene, *The Elegant Universe* (New York: W.W. Norton, 2010).
- Brian Greene, *Until the End of Time* (New York: Alfred A. Knopf, 2020).
- Stephen Hawking and Leonard Mlodinow, *The Grand Design* (New York: Bantam Books, 2010).
- Sabine Hossenfelder, *Lost in Math: How Beauty Leads Physics Astray* (New York: Basic Books, 2018).
- Sabine Hossenfelder, *Existential Physics* (New York: Viking, 2022).
- Michio Kaku, *Parallel Worlds: A Journey through Creation, Higher Dimensions, and the Future of the Cosmos* (New York: Anchor Books, 2006).
- Michio Kaku, *The God Equation: The Quest for a Theory of Everything* (New York: Anchor Books, 2021).
- Carlo Rovelli, *Reality Is not What it Seems: The Journey to Quantum Gravity* (New York: Penguin Random House, 2017).
- Carlo Rovelli, *Seven Brief Lessons on Physics* (New York: Penguin Random House, 2016).
- Lee Smolin, *Einstein's Unfinished Revolution: The Search for What Lies Beyond the Quantum* (New York: Penguin Random House, 2019).

If you would like to find out more about Wisdom teachings, these books are a good start:

- Cynthia Bourgeault, *The Wisdom Jesus: Transforming Heart and Mind—a New Perspective on Christ and His Message* (Boston: Shambala, 2008).
- Cynthia Bourgeault, *The Wisdom Way of Knowing: Reclaiming an Ancient Tradition to Awaken the Heart* (San Francisco: John Wiley & Sons, 2003).
- Kabir Helminski, *Living Presence: The Sufi Path to Mindfulness and the Essential Self* (New York: Penguin Random House, 2017).
- Naomi Levy, *Einstein and the Rabbi: Searching for the Soul* (New York: Flatiron Books, (2017).
- Thomas Merton, *New Seeds of Contemplation* (New York: New Directions, 2007).
- Tenzin Wangyal Rinpoche, *Tibetan Yogas of Body, Speech and Mind* (Ithaca, New York: Snow Lion Publications, 2011).
- Chogyal Namkhai Norbu, *Dzogchen, the Self-Perfected State* (Ithaca NY: Snow Lion Publications, 2000).

An excellent site to find out more about the Christian Wisdom tradition and path is Wisdom Waypoints: https://wisdomwaypoints.org/. There are also Wisdom Schools available online, through the Center for Action and Contemplation. https://cac.org/online-ed/course-catalog/; Cynthia Bourgeault's Introductory Wisdom School https://cac.org/introductory-wisdom-school/; Divine Exchange https://cac.org/the-divine-exchange/; and Mary Magdalene: Apostle to Our Own Times https://cac.org/online-education/mary-magdalene/, to name just a few.

For more on Centering Prayer, a good place to start is with these books by Cynthia Bourgeault and Father Thomas Keating. There is also much more information on the Contemplative Outreach site, www.contemplativeoutreach.org:

- Cynthia Bourgeault, *Centering Prayer and Inner Awakening* (Lanham MD: Cowley Publications, 2004).

- Cynthia Bourgeault, *The Heart of Centering Prayer: Nondual Christianity in Theory and Practice* (Boulder: Shambhala, 2016).
- Thomas Keating, *Invitation to Love* (New York: Bloomsbury Continuum; 20th anniversary edition, 2012).
- Thomas Keating, *Open Mind, Open Heart: The Contemplative Dimension of the Gospel* (New York: Bloomsbury Continuum, 2019).

If you are seeking a spiritual director, someone who can be a companion for you on your spiritual path, in whatever form it may take, find out more at Spiritual Directors International, https://www.sdicompanions.org/. They have a searchable directory to help you find a companion who is a good match for you.

About the Author

Joy Andrews Hayter is a scientist, contemplative, and lover of nature and the arts. As professor emerita of physical chemistry at California State University East Bay, and former staff scientist researcher at Stanford University's SLAC National Laboratory, she taught quantum mechanics and its applications to chemistry, and used leading-edge tools of X-ray physics to study alternative energy solutions and environmental remediation. She has co-authored over seventy academic publications, and has presented plenary and invited talks on several continents.

Joy spends more of her time these days as a spiritual director, a companion to people in their search to find a deeper relationship with the divine indwelling. She teaches Centering Prayer and other contemplative practices. She leads and facilitates meditations, retreats, quiet days, and mindfulness classes. She has published articles on science and spirituality and on Centering Prayer in periodicals for the Centering Prayer and spiritual direction communities, and contributes to a regular Q&A column on Centering Prayer. She lives in Northern California with her husband Paul. You can contact Joy via her website: joyfullfillment.com.

Notes

[1] Excerpt from Rumi, "Great Wagon" in *The Essential Rumi*, trans. Coleman Barks (New York: Harper One, 2004), 35-37.

[2] Fritjov Capra, *The Tao of Physics* (Boston: Shambhala, 1975).

[3] I'm sure there are ways of doing this without going cross-eyed. In any case, the meditation I practice now does not suggest that.

[4] Steven Tainer is a gifted Buddhist teacher. He did much of the writing for Tibetan Buddhist Tarthang Tulku Rinpoche's books, including his 1977 book, *Time, Space and Knowledge: A New Vision of Reality.*

[5] You can read much more on this in Cynthia Bourgeault, *The Wisdom Jesus: Transforming Heart and Mind—A New Perspective on Christ and His Message* (Boston: Shambala, 2008).

[6] Cynthia Bourgeault emphasizes this in *The Wisdom Jesus*, 31.

[7] These translations are from Janet M. Magiera, *Aramaic Peshitta New Testament: Dictionary Number Lexicon* (Colorado Springs: Light of the Word Ministry, 2009), 13. The Aramaic version of the New Testament I use in this book is the Peshitta, a version of the Old and New Testaments in Syriac, which is a dialect of Eastern Aramaic. Some people maintain that the New Testament Peshitta evolved from original sources written in Aramaic, and others maintain that Peshitta is a translation from Greek texts back to Aramaic. But being that there are far fewer words in Aramaic, it is far easier to back translate than any forward translation which may have occurred. As with many older languages, many words in Aramaic have multiple meanings, lending to several levels of interpretation. (Those who have ears to hear, let them hear.) We know Jesus spoke Aramaic, the *lingua franca* of his time, because there are multiple instances in the New Testament in which the original Aramaic is included, e.g. *"Talitha cumi"* ("maiden arise," Mark 5:41)

and "*Eli Eli lama sabachthani*" ("my God, my God, why have you forsaken me," Matthew 27:46, similar in Mark 15:34).

[8] Thomas Merton, *Conjectures of a Guilty Bystander* (New York: Image, 2016), 153-54.

[9] Merton, *Conjectures of a Guilty Bystander*, 156.

[10] Sometimes called "The Big Mama of All Fields," the Higgs field gives rise to the Higgs boson, detected in 2012 at the Large Hadron Collider (LHC) at CERN in Switzerland. The Higgs field is also said to contain all the other fields that give rise to other particles.

[11] The protons and neutrons in the dense nuclei of atoms are made of smaller particles called quarks that are more space than substance as well. The word quark comes from a line in James Joyce's *Finnegan's Wake*, "Three quarks for Muster Mark." Quarks are named as different "flavors" such as up, down, strange, charm, top, and bottom; and "colors" such as red, blue, and green that do not correspond to real colors, but are convenient labels to distinguish them. But quarks do not really take up space either. They can be viewed as "point" particles or, in string theory, as excitations of tiny strings that don't take up any volume.

[12] The Planck length is 1.6×10^{-35} meters. This is extremely small: the relative size of the Planck scale to a miniscule atom (10^{-10} meters) is about the same as the relative size of a person (1 meter) to the entire observable universe with all its galaxies etc. (10^{27} meters).

[13] Sean Carroll, *Something Deeply Hidden: Quantum Worlds and the Emergence of Spacetime* (New York: Penguin Random House, 2019), 36.

[14] This is from Cynthia Bourgeault's course, "The Divine Exchange" offered by the Center for Action and Contemplation, found on their website.

[15] Richard P. Feynman, *QED: The Strange Theory of Light and Matter* (Princeton, NJ: Princeton University Press, 1985), 9.

[16] As described by Tibetan Buddhist (Dzogchen) master Chogyal Namkhai Norbu.

[17] Cynthia Bourgeault, *The Wisdom Way of Knowing: Reclaiming an Ancient Tradition to Awaken the Heart* (San Francisco: John Wiley & Sons, 2003), xvii.

[18] See e.g. Matthew 24:43, 25:13, 26:38-41, and Mark 14:34-38.

[19] Albert Einstein as quoted in Max Born, *Physik im Wandel Meiner Zeit* (Braunschweig: Vieweg, 1966).

[20] Kabir Helminski, *Living Presence: The Sufi Path to Mindfulness and the Essential Self* (New York: Tarcher Perigee, 2017), 205.

[21] These three verses are from John 14:20, John 15:5, and John 15:9, respectively, New Revised Standard Version.

[22] French physicist Louis de Broglie studied the wave nature of particles and found that the wavelength for any matter is given by the equation $\lambda = h/mv$, where λ is the wavelength, h is Planck's constant (a very small number, 6.626 x 10^{-34} J•s), m is the mass and v is the velocity of the particle). The wavelength for things with larger mass, like baseballs and cats, is very small compared to their physical size, so it is indiscernible on that larger scale. But the wavelength of an electron in a hydrogen (H) atom corresponds exactly to the circumference of its wave-shape around the nucleus, making it quite relevant for the atom: the de Broglie wavelength of the H electron in its ground state, with speed 2200 km/s, is 3.3×10^{-10} m, or 0.33 nm. This length corresponds to the circumference ($2\pi r$) of the first Bohr radius of the H atom. With radius 0.053 nm the circumference would be 0.33 nm and so its de Broglie wavelength is quite relevant.

[23] Where two peaks are added together in a way that their peaks coincide it's called constructive interference and we see a smear of light. Where the two wave patterns meet with their peaks and troughs in opposite directions, they cancel each other out (destructive interference) and we see dark areas in the interference pattern.

[24] The strangeness of the double slit experiment becomes more apparent if only one photon is sent through the slits at a time. The single photon wave will pass through *both* slits at the same time! It then appears as a single dot on the detector made by the photon particle hitting the screen. As more single photons are sent through, the single photon particles fill out an interference pattern in the figure, the same type of interference pattern we would see for a wave. Each photon hits the screen as a particle, but multiple particles still show up on the screen in a wave interference pattern, indicating that the photon went through both slits as a wave. Hence even a single photon behaves as both particle and wave!

[25] This is called the photoelectric effect, explained by Einstein in 1905.

[26] Heisenberg's uncertainty principle says that if you know the position (of a particle) precisely, the momentum gets more undefined, and vice versa. This

is written $\Delta p \Delta x \geq \hbar$ where p is momentum, x is position, Δp and Δx are the uncertainties and $\hbar$ is Planck's constant, a very tiny number.

[27] See His Holiness the Dalai Lama, *The Universe in a Single Atom: The Convergence of Science and Spirituality* (New York: Harmony Books, 2005), 63.

[28] Dalai Lama, "A Buddhist Concept of Nature," transcript of an address on February 4, 1992, at New Delhi, India, available at dalailama.com.

[29] Cynthia Bourgeault, *The Wisdom Way of Knowing*, 47.

[30] Feynman's method is called the path-integral formulation, or sum-over-histories approach. In Feynman's approach, the particle takes an infinite number of paths to get to its destination. The overall pattern of those paths looks like a wave (creating an interference pattern as seen earlier). Each electron ends up in a single place upon collision with a detector in our 4D spacetime, but the overall pattern it makes is that of a wave. Some electron paths are more likely, though, and we are more likely to observe the results of those paths. Hence the bright bands of the interference pattern.

[31] Christophe Galfard, *The Universe in Your Hand: A Journey through Space, Time and Beyond* (New York: Flatiron Books, 2016), 213.

[32] Richard P. Feynman, *QED*, 9.

[33] For a review of this see H. Y. Huang et al., "Quantum Advantage in Learning From Experiments," *Science* 376, no. 6598 (2022): 1182-86.

[34] This mixture happens at a unique pressure and temperature called the triple point.

[35] See e.g. an experiment at the SLAC LCLS; J.M. Glownia, et al., "Self-Referenced Coherent Diffraction X-Ray Movie of Ångstrom- and Femtosecond-Scale Atomic Motion," *Physical Review Letters* 117 (2016): 153003.

[36] The classical concept of probability more familiar to us is different from the quantum "probability wave." In the classical case, if I roll two dice there is a certain probability that I will come up with "snake eyes" (two ones). In this type of probability, we take it for granted that the dice are objects the whole time, even if the person rolling them puts them behind her back and we don't see them while she shakes them. However, in the quantum situation the "dice," or the particles, don't manifest until they hit the detector—until we observe them. Before hitting the detector the "particle" exists as the superposition of all

its possibilities. Or they live outside of our 4D spacetime, more like the super time-traveling electrons described by Feynman.

[37] For more about the "many worlds" theory and its interpretation, see Sean Carroll, *Something Deeply Hidden: Quantum Worlds and the Emergence of Spacetime* (New York: Penguin Random House, 2019).

[38] Cynthia Bourgeault, *Eye of the Heart: A Spiritual Journey into the Imaginal Realm* (Boulder, CO: Shambhala, 2020).

[39] Sean Carroll, *Something Deeply Hidden*, 234.

[40] Gospel of Thomas, Logion 17. This particular translation is from Lynn C. Bauman, Ward J. Bauman, and Cynthia Bourgeault, *The Luminous Gospels* (Telephone, TX: Praxis Publishing, 2008), 14.

[41] This hypothetical experiment with a cat makes no sense on our macro-scale. The cat would be in an unknown alive/dead state initially along with the decayed/undecayed radioactive atom, but once the gas was triggered it would already be dead, whether we observed it or not. (Bohr's interpretation would agree with that.) The encounter with the macroworld would be earlier, e.g. with the gas. Schrödinger set up this experiment to show that the Copenhagen interpretation, where the observer collapses the wavefunction, made no sense. The ensuing debate initiated the many worlds interpretation.

[42] For example, scientists at Stanford's SLAC National Laboratory accomplished a Schrödinger's cat-type experiment using a powerful free electron laser, the Linac Coherent Light Source (LCLS). They placed iodine molecules, which have one single bond between two iodine atoms, into the powerful laser beam. They were able to make movies showing that a single molecule did two things at the same time: it (1) stayed in the ground state (which is less reactive) and did not react, and also (2) was excited and split into two separate iodine atoms. The interference between the two states, much as seen earlier in the double slit experiment, confirmed that a single iodine molecule was in *both states at the same time*. This is one of the many experiments that confirm a real live Schrödinger's "cat" state—in this case "cat"-type iodine molecules. See J. M. Glownia et al., 2016.

[43] These quantum states have impressive and odd properties, but they are not being done on the macroscale, or even at typical temperatures (the atoms were

very cold, to get them all into the same state). See Jacob Aron, "New Quantum Record as Ball of Atoms Ends Up in Two Spots at Once," *New Scientist*, December 28, 2015. From academic article by T. Kovatchy, et al., "Quantum Superposition at the Half-Metre Scale," *Nature*, 528 (2015): 530-33.

[44] See for example two journal articles in *Science*, by Forschungszentrum Juelich, described in *ScienceDaily*, August, 2019.

[45] See Yale University, *Science News*, June 3, 2019, "Physicists Can Predict the Jumps of Schrödinger's Cat (and Finally Save It)," at sciencedaily.com; also Z. K. Minev, S. O. Mundhada, S. Shankar, P. Reinhold, R. Gutiérrez-Jáuregui, R. J. Schoelkopf, M. Mirrahimi, H. J. Carmichael, M. H. Devoret, "To Catch and Reverse a Quantum Jump Mid-Flight," *Nature*, 570, (2019): 200-4.

[46] C. T. Rodgers, P. J. Hore, "Chemical magnetoreception in birds: The radical pair mechanism," *Proc. Natl. Acad. Sci.* 106 (2009): 353–60.

[47] They were polarized paired photons. For a movie describing this see Gabriel Popkin, "China's Quantum Satellite Achieves 'Spooky Action' at Record Distance," *Science News*, June 15, 2017 ; also Juan Yin et al., "Satellite-Based Entanglement Distribution Over 1200 Kilometers," *Science*, 356 (2017):1140-44.

[48] This was facilitated by advances in data processing as well, to sort out the extensive data set. See University of Geneva, "A Single Photon Reveals Quantum Entanglement of 16 Million Atoms," Phys Org, October 13, 2017, at phys.org; also Florian Fröwis et al. "Experimental certification of millions of genuinely entangled atoms in a solid," *Nature Communications* 8 (2017): 907.

[49] See Adrian Cho, "Quantum Internet Closer as Physicists Stretch Spooky Link Between Atoms," *Science News*, February 13, 2020, at sciencemag.org; also Y. Yu, F. Ma, X. Luo, et al., "Entanglement of Two Quantum Memories Via Fibres Over Dozens of Kilometres," *Nature* 578 (2020): 240–45.

[50] See David Nield, "Physicists Just Achieved the First-Ever Quantum Teleportation Between Computer Chips," Science Alerts, December 31, 2019, at sciencealert.com; also D. Llewellyn, Y. Ding, I. I. Faruque, et al., "Chip-to-Chip Quantum Teleportation and Multi-Photon Entanglement in Silicon," *Nature Physics* 16 (2020): 148-53.

[51] K. G. Fedorov et al., "Experimental Quantum Teleportation of Propagating Microwaves," *Science Advances* 7, no. 52 (2021): eabk0891.

[52] See Fiona Macdonald, "Physicists Just Achieved Quantum Teleportation Underwater for the First Time," Science Alert, August 28, 2017, at sciencealert.com; also Ling Ji et al., "Towards Quantum Communications in Free-Space Seawater," *Optics Express* 25, no. 17 (2017):19795-806.

[53] Philip Ball, "Quantum Teleportation Is Even Weirder than You Think," Nature.com, July 20, 2017; also Ji-Gang Ren et al, "Ground-To-Satellite Quantum Teleportation," *Nature* 549 (2017): 70-73.

[54] As translated in Daniel Ladinsky, *Love Poems from God: Twelve Sacred Voices from the East and West* (New York: Penguin, 2002), 72.

[55] This saying by Quaker George Fox (1652; Epistle, #19, Works 7:27) was used by Paulette Meier to create a chant with these words.

[56] See e.g. A.J. Heinrich, W. D. Oliver, L.M.K. Vandersypen, et al., "Quantum-Coherent Nanoscience," *Nature Nanotechnology* 16 (2021): 1318-29.

[57] Quantum effects in biology have often been reviewed in recent years, including articles in highly respected journals such as *Nature* and *Nature Physics*. A review that covers a lot of these is Y. Kim, F. Bertagna, E.M. D'Souza, D.J. Heyes, L.O. Johannissen, E.T. Nery, A. Pantelias, A. Sanchez-Pedreño Jimenez, L. Slocombe, M.G. Spencer, et al., "Quantum Biology: An Update and Perspective," *Quantum Reports* 3 (2021): 1-48.

[58] Superconductors have zero electrical resistance and repel magnetic fields. This is how the trains and other materials made with superconductors can levitate.

[59] Prototypes have been made, but currently they are not practical because they require lots of liquid nitrogen and special surfaces to operate.

[60] Matter made of fermions can form "composite bosons" when particles such as electrons, which are fermions and can't occupy the same space at the same time, combine in pairs to make bosons. These composite bosons can behave more in sync, as one continuous whole.

[61] When looking at Hebrew biblical texts translated into English, more than one word in the original version is translated as "mercy." For example, the Hebrew word *chesed* is often translated as mercy, but also as kindness, goodness, and lovingkindness. *Chesed* also implies commitment, loyalty, or faithfulness within a marriage or community. In the Beatitudes (Matthew 5:5) the Peshitta uses the word *rahme*, which is translated as mercy or compassion.

[62] It is said that Archbishop Sijeric the Serious made a pilgrimage along the Via Francigena from Canterbury to Rome back in 990 C.E. to meet with Pope John XV to be ordained.

[63] Taizé is a type of prayerful chant originating in the ecumenical Taizé monastery in Burgundy, France.

[64] See e.g. Stephen W. Porges et al., "Cardiac Vagal Tone: A Neurophysiological Mechanism That Evolved in Mammals to Dampen Threat Reactions and Promote Sociality," *World Psychiatry* 20, no. 2 (2021):, 296-98. See also books on polyvagal theory by Porges, and by D. Dana.

[65] Stephen W. Porges, 2021. This has also been studied by the HeartMath Institute, as described e.g. in R. McCraty, M. Atkinson, D. Tomasino, T. Bradley, "The Coherent Heart: Heart–Brain Interactions, Psychophysiological Coherence, and the Emergence of System-Wide Order," *Integral Review* 5 (2009): 11–115.

[66] See for example Pierre Teilhard de Chardin, *The Human Phenomenon.* A new edition and translation by Sarah Appleton-Weber (Eastbourne UK, Sussex Academic Press, 1999, 2003, 2015).

[67] Hafiz, "Forgive the Dream," in *The Gift,* trans. Daniel Ladinsky (New York: Penguin, 1999), 125-26.

[68] As translated in Daniel Ladinsky, *Love Poems from God*, 274.

[69] Daniel Ladinsky, *Love Poems from God*, 274.

[70] Participles in Aramaic can act as nouns, adjectives, or verbs, depending on context.

[71] Pierre Teilhard de Chardin, "The Evolution of Chastity," in *Toward the Future,* trans. Rene Hague (New York: Harcourt, 1975), 60.

[72] The Higgs boson was obtained by colliding two proton beams at nearly the speed of light. The Higgs boson has a mass of about 126 GeV/c^2, or about 126 times the mass of a proton, one of the building blocks of matter that can be found in the nuclei of atoms. We'll read more about it later in this chapter.

[73] One gram of mass would produce $E = mc^2$, or $\{(1\ g) \times (1\ kg/1000\ g) \times (3 \times 10^8\ m/s)^2 =\}$ 9.0×10^{13} Joules of energy. $(1\ J = kg\ m^2/s^2)$ Then for a 150 W device $(1\ W = 1\ J\ s^{-1}$ or $1\ J$ per second) we have enough energy to light it a long time: $[9.0 \times 10^{13}\ J/(150\ J\ s^{-1})] \times (1\ h/3600\ s) \times (1\ day/24\ h) \times (1\ year/365\ days) = 19$ thousand years. That's a lot of energy from half a dime! In reality nuclear reactions

do not convert every bit of mass to energy: they produce slightly less massive particles, but even this slight loss of mass still releases a lot of energy.

[74] In one 2009 study, scientists documented faint bioluminescence from the human body, presumably due to our metabolism. Journal article: M. Kobayashi, D. Kikuchi, H. Okamura, "Imaging of Ultraweak Spontaneous Photon Emission from Human Body Displaying Diurnal Rhythm," *PLoS ONE* 4, no.7 (2009): e6256.

[75] W. Meacham, J.E. Alcock, R. Bucklin, K.O.L. Burridge, J.R. Cole, R.J. Dent, J.P. Jackson, W.C. McCrone, P.C. Maloney, M.M. Mueller, J. Nickell, A.J. Otterbein, S.F. Pellicori, S. Schafersman, G. Tamburelli, and A.D. Whanger, "The Authentication of the Turin Shroud: An Issue in Archaeological Epistemology" [and Comments and Reply], *Current Anthropology*, 24, no.3 (1983), 283–311.

[76] The light proposed is in the far ultraviolet. See e.g. : P. Di Lazzaro, D. Murra, E. Nichelatti, A. Santoni, and G. Baldacchini, "Superficial and Shroud-Like Coloration of Linen by Short Laser Pulses in the Vacuum Ultraviolet," *Applied Optics* 51 (2012): 8567-78.

[77] C.M. Wilson, G. Johansson, A. Pourkabirian, M. Simoen, J.R. Johansson, T. Duty, F. Nori, and P. Delsing, "Observation of the dynamical Casimir effect in a superconducting circuit," *Nature*, 47 (2011): 376–79. Read more at: https://phys.org/news/2011-11-scientists-vacuum.html. Many similar experiments have been accomplished since then as well.

[78] As seen earlier with the slit experiment, Heisenberg's uncertainty principle says that if you know the momentum (of a particle) precisely, the position gets more "spread out." This is written $\Delta p \Delta x \geq \hbar$ where p is momentum, x is position, Δp and Δx are the uncertainties and $\hbar$ is Planck's constant, a very tiny number. Energy also becomes increasingly indefinite as its position becomes more definite, as space is constrained.

[79] Creation and annihilation operators are commonly used in a particular system of quantum mechanics, but at that point I just hadn't encountered this type of formulation or terminology.

[80] The exchange of virtual particles can also occur between two particles of opposite charge, causing attraction. The virtual particles act more like "messenger" particles than heavy rocks or snowballs – they transmit the message of attraction or repulsion.

[81] This actually only happens when we observe it, much as the particle-wave only collapsed into a single location when we observed it with a detector. If we stick with austere quantum mechanics, in quantum field theory the vacuum is empty and serene. It's only when we try to look at very small areas that we see the effects of the Heisenberg Uncertainty principle and particles appear. In other words it's a lot like what we saw with the slit experiment: when we look for a particle, a particle is what we find. See discussion in Sean Carroll, *Something Deeply Hidden: Quantum Worlds and the Emergence of Spacetime* (New York: Penguin Random House, 2019), chapter 12 on quantum field theory.

[82] C.M. Wilson et al., "Observation of the Dynamical Casimir Effect in a Superconducting Circuit," *Nature* 479 (2011): 376-79. Read more at: https://phys.org/news/2011-11-scientists-vacuum.html

[83] Sean Carroll, *Something Deeply Hidden*, 264.

[84] Unlike Schrödinger's formulation for quantum mechanics that has been used for many calculations on atoms and molecules, QFT can deal with particles moving near or at the speed of light, including photons, because it also accounts for relativity. QFT can also work with large numbers of particles at a time, much more suitable for large molecules and ensembles of them.

When Erwin Schrödinger first came up with the equations used by chemists and others to model the quantum mechanics of molecules, he didn't take Einstein's theory of special relativity into account. His formalism was adequate for orbitals around atoms and molecules but in an awkward fashion, attempting to account for all the particles (i.e. electrons, protons, and neutrons) separately. This is almost as if the company supplying water to my house wanted to track every drop of water as it entered the house and left through the wastewater system or the garden, rather than just knowing how many gallons I had used. It would take too much time, without adding useful information.

[85] Via a phenomenon physicists call "symmetry breaking."

[86] Rapped by science journalist Kate McAlpine (@alpinekat on YouTube). She starts to rap about the Higgs about half way through. https://www.youtube.com/watch?v=j50ZssEojtM

[87] From Mahayana Buddhism.

[88] Vibrations of the quark fields make the quarks within protons and neutrons, and vibrations of the gluon field form the gluons that hold the quarks together.

[89] Physicists tell us that a completely empty vacuum would be quite unstable. For a great simulation of particles constantly being created and destroyed see YouTube video, "Empty Space is NOT Empty."

[90] See Ethan Siegel, "This is Why Physicists Think String Theory Might Be the Theory of Everything," *Forbes,* May 31, 2018.

[91] Vibrating strings at a tiny level help to "smooth" out the huge energy spikes we would see if particles occupied only a single point (remember the Heisenberg Uncertainty Principle says that when space is confined, energy becomes wildly unpredictable), helping these two theories to mesh together. For more about string theory see writings by physicists Michio Kaku, Brian Greene, and Stephen Hawking.

[92] Sabine Hossenfelder, *Lost in Math: How Beauty Leads Physics Astray* (New York: Hachette Book Group, 2018), 188.

[93] The Planck length is 1.6 x 10^{-35} meters. This is extremely small: the relative size of the Planck scale to a miniscule atom (10^{-10} meters) is about the same as the relative size of a person (1 meter) to the entire universe with all its galaxies etc. (10^{25} meters). Recall that because of the Heisenberg Uncertainty Principle, when distance is very small energy becomes highly unpredictable. By introducing vibrating strings of finite length rather than point particles without length, the resulting energy spikes were not as much an issue.

[94] Part of the mystery is that, unlike QFT, M-theory does not presume spacetime as a given fundamental existence, but that it emerges only in specific conditions. See the Introduction in Becker, K., Becker, M. & Schwartz, J.H. *String Theory and M-Theory: A Modern Introduction.* Cambridge: Cambridge University Press, 2007. p. 12.

[95] According to physicist Edward Witten, M theory includes membranes as well as strings.

[96] Excerpted from Michio Kaku's YouTube video, "The Multiverse has 11 Dimensions."

[97] They fall generally into a form called Calabi-Yau. A 2D projection of a different Calabi-Yau space is on the cover of this book.

[98] This analogy was used by Brian Greene in *The Elegant Universe* (New York: W.W. Norton, 2010), 186.

[99] One dimension is along the length of the wire, and the second follows a circle

along each point in the wire. In this case we have something closer to a 3D object such as a thin hose, but described with just two dimensions, like a 2D sheet of paper rolled up to make a tube.

[100] See Barbara Brown Taylor, *The Luminous Web: Essays on Science and Religion* (Washington DC: Rowman & Littlefield, 2000).

[101] Francis H. Cook, *Hua-Yen Buddhism: The Jewel Net of Indra* (University Park, PA: Penn State Press, 1977).

[102] John 14:20, New Revised Standard Version.

[103] See miegakure.com. Also, much as the blind men perceived just a portion of the elephant as they encountered it, depending on which part they touched, we can also visualize an object in four spatial dimensions by viewing parts of it as it dips into 3D space. We can't view the whole thing, but perceive only a partial picture. When we try to visualize a tesseract, which is cube-like but exists in four spatial dimensions rather than three, we see different shapes as it projects into 3D space.

[104] See the YouTube Video, "How to walk through walls using the 4th Dimension."

[105] Michio Kaku, *Parallel Worlds: A Journey Through Creation, Higher Dimensions, and the Future of the Cosmos* (New York: Anchor Books, 2006).

[106] For example, see Stephen Hawking and Leonard Mlodinow, *The Grand Design* (New York: Bantam Books, 2010).

[107] Gebser's views are discussed by Jeremy Johnson in *Seeing Through the Worlds: Jean Gebser and Integral Consciousness* (Seattle WA: Revelore Press, 2019).

[108] The cold outer universe is just 2.7 degrees Celsius above absolute zero, the coldest temperature possible, which is -273.15 degrees Celsius or −459.67 degrees Fahrenheit.

[109] Sean Carroll, *Something Deeply Hidden: Quantum Worlds and the Emergence of Spacetime* (New York: Penguin Random House, 2019), 36.

[110] See e.g. the story "A Cup of Tea" in Paul Reps and Nyogen Senzaki, *Zen Flesh, Zen Bones: A Collection of Zen and Pre-Zen Writings* (Boston: Tuttle, 1985), 19.

[111] For more about these hidden agendas, called "emotional programs for happiness," see Thomas Keating, *Invitation to Love: The Way of Christian Contemplation* (London: Bloomsbury, 2012), 6-16.

[112] From a radio interview with Martin Redfern, as quoted by Marina Jones in "John Wheeler's Participatory Universe," February 13, 2014, at futurism.com.

[113] P. Moors, J. Wagemans, L. de-Wit, "Causal events enter awareness faster than non-causal events," *Peer J* (2017): e2932.

[114] The perceptive processing of causal events occurs more quickly than for non-causal events, e.g. for the second and third cases that are not at all how billiard balls behave.

[115] A link to inherent bias tests at Harvard, with respect to our unconscious biases regarding, for example: Asians, weight, sexuality, weapons, disability, gender, Arab-Muslims, age, presidents, skin-tone, and religion is found at implicit.harvard.edu.

[116] The parietal lobe is particularly important in the formation of our sense of being a separate self. For information on the various parts of the brain and their main roles, see Andrew Newberg and Mark Robert Waldman, *How God Changes Your Brain: Breakthrough Findings from a Leading Neuroscientist* (New York: Ballantine Books, 2010). A table on p. 43 summarizes functions of various parts of the brain.

[117] D.D. Hoffman, M. Singh, P. Prakash, "The Interface Theory of Perception," *Psychonomic Bulletin Review* 22 (2015): 1480-1506.

[118] Neil deGrasse Tyson, *Astrophysics for People in a Hurry* (New York: W.W. Norton, 2017), 196-97.

[119] Beatrice Bruteau, "Prayer and Identity," *Contemplative Review* 16, no.3 (1983): 2-17.

[120] Lewis Keizer, a former Episcopal priest and biblical scholar who studies the historical teachings of Jesus, discussed the meaning of the term *olam* in the context of the Kabbalah, the mystical arm of Judaism. He said *olam*, which would be *aeon* in Greek, is a "Kabbalistic term meaning Age, Aeon, Era, World. A state of existence." From Lewis Keizer, *The Gospel of Yeshua* (Coppell TX: Independently published, 2021), 59.

[121] Cynthia Bourgeault, *The Wisdom Jesus*, 30.

[122] In his foreword to Bayo Akomolafe, *These Wilds Beyond Our Fences* (Berkeley, CA: North Atlantic Books, 2017).

[123] Quote taken from Bayo Akomolafe's personal website: bayoakomolafe.net/about/.

[124] Kabir Helminski, *Living Presence*, 44.

[125] Jon Kabat-Zinn, *Wherever You Go, There You Are* (New York: Hachette Books, 2014), 86.

[126] See Robert Sardello, *Heartfulness* (La Veta, CO: Goldenstone Press, 2017).

[127] Cynthia Bourgeault, for example, describes the egoic (binary) and unitive operating systems in *The Wisdom Jesus*, 33-40.

[128] Chogyal Namkhai Norbu, *Dzogchen: The Self-Perfected State* (Ithaca NY: Snow Lion Publications, 2000), 30.

[129] Richard Rohr, *The Universal Christ: How a Forgotten Reality Can Change Everything We See, Hope For, and Believe* (New York: Convergent Books, 2019), 209.

[130] Andrew Newberg & Mark Robert Waldman, *How God Changes Your Brain*, 2010.

[131] Professor of Psychiatry and Psychology at the University of Wisconsin, Madison.

[132] Ten thousand hours is the amount of time Malcolm Gladwell claims we need to become experts on anything. See Malcolm Gladwell, *Outliers: The Story of Success* (New York: Little, Brown, 2008).

[133] Gamma brain waves were ignored for a long time in EEG studies. They are very high frequency and can be lost in "the noise." They are associated with synchrony among various areas of the brain, involving synthesis and "aha" moments, and are thought to be related to a state of conscious attention. Other imaging studies of meditators also show long-range gamma waves synchronization, for example A. Berkovich-Ohana, "A Case Study of a Meditation-Induced Altered State: Increased Overall Gamma Synchronization," *Phenomenology and the Cognitive Sciences*, 16, no. 1 (2017): 91-106.

[134] A. Lutz, L. L. Grelschar, N. B. Rawlings, M. Ricard, R. J. Davidson, "Long-Term Meditators Self-Induce High-Amplitude Gamma Synchrony During Mental Practice," Proceedings of the National Academy of Science 101 (2004): 16369–73. Copyright (2004) National Academy of Sciences, U.S.A.

[135] Daniel Goleman and Richard J. Davidson, *Altered Traits: Science Reveals How Meditation Changes Your Mind, Brain, and Body* (New York: Random House, 2017), 245.

[136] This effect is also described in a chapter called "The After is the Before for the Next During," in Goleman and Richardson's *Altered Traits*.

[137] In the discussion section of the paper the authors wrote: "Our study shows that a short meditation intervention in trained subjects rapidly influenced the methylome at sites of potential clinical relevance, related to the transcriptional regulation of the inflammation response, immune cell metabolism, DNA repair, cell aging, RNA metabolism, protein translation, cell adhesion and neurotransmission." See R. Chaix, M. Fabny, M. Cosin- Tomás, M. Alvarez-López, L. Lemee, B. Regnault, R. Davidson, A. Lutz, A. and P. Kaliman, "Differential DNA Methylation in Experienced Meditators After an Intensive Day of Mindfulness-Based Practice: Implications for Immune-Related Pathways," *Brain, Behavior and Immunity* 84 (2020): 36-44.

[138] For a summary of long-term effects of meditation and mindfulness see Bob Stahl and Elisha Goldstein, *A Mindfulness Based Stress Reduction Workbook* (Oakland, CA: New Harbinger Publications, 2010), 30-32; Daniel Goleman and Richard J. Davidson, *Altered Traits*; and Daniel J. Siegel, *The Mindful Brain: Reflection and Attunement in the Cultivation of Well-Being* (New York: W.W. Norton, 2007).

[139] In "Buddha at the Gas Pump," podcast 420, October 3, 2017, at batgap.com.

[140] This is from Janet M. Magiera, *Aramaic Peshitta New Testament: Dictionary Number Lexicon* (Colorado Springs: Light of the Word Ministry, 2009), 108.

[141] This handy concordance/lexicon accounts for each word in the Bible by number, for cross-referencing translations in Greek and Hebrew.

[142] Adapted from James Finley, *The Contemplative Heart* (Notre Dame, IN: Sorin Books, 2000), 125-26.

[143] Barbara A. Holmes, *Joy Unspeakable: Contemplative Practices of the Black Church, 2nd Edition* (Minneapolis: Fortress Press, 2017), xx.

[144] Viktor E. Frankl, *Man's Search for Meaning* (Boston: Beacon Press, 2006), 66.

[145] As quoted in Paul Davies, *God and the New Physics* (New York: Simon & Schuster, 1992).

[146] Thomas Merton, *Conjectures of a Guilty Bystander*, 153-55.

[147] Cynthia Bourgeault, *Mystical Hope: Trusting in the Mercy of God* (Cambridge MA: Cowley Publications, 2001), 84.

[148] James Finley, *Intimacy: The Divine Ambush* (Albuquerque NM: Center for Action and Contemplation, 2013).

[149] Lewis Keizer, *The Gospel of Yeshua* (Coppell TX: Independently published, 2021), 20.

[150] Thomas Keating, *From the Mind to the Heart.* (Temple Rock Company, 2017). Pages are not numbered. Available from Contemplative Outreach (contemplative outreach.org). Thomas Keating passed away in 2018.

[151] Nancy Manahan and Becky Bohan, *Living Consciously, Dying Gracefully: A Journey With Cancer and Beyond* (Edina, MN: Beaver's Pond Press, 2007). See Chapter 14, "The Portal."

[152] See Cynthia Bourgeault, *Eye of the Heart: A Spiritual Journey into the Imaginal Realm* (Boulder, CO: Shambhala Publications, Inc., 2020), 21-22.

[153] Bin Yan and Nikolai A. Sinitsyn "Recovery of Damaged Information and the Out-of-Time-Ordered Correlators." *Physical Review Lett*ers 125 (2020): 040605.

[154] The Hebrew word of the same root, shmaya, can literally mean the visible heavens or sky, but also directly the abode of God, not necessarily a physical place (See Strong's Hebrew Concordance H8064, available online). The word is also sometimes used as a metonymy where heaven refers to God.

[155] See Neil Douglas-Klotz, *The Hidden Gospel: Decoding the Spiritual Message of the Aramaic Jesus* (Wheaton IL: Quest Books, 1999), 100.

[156] Thomas Merton, *Conjectures of a Guilty Bystander*, 155-56.

[157] Richard Rohr, "The Cosmic Christ," Center for Action and Contemplation, November 5, 2015. Also see Richard Rohr, *The Universal Christ*, 2019.

[158] 1 Corinthians 12:12-14, 20-27, New Revised Standard Version

[159] Gospel of Thomas, Logion 77. This particular translation is from Lynn C. Bauman, Ward J. Bauman, and Cynthia Bourgeault, *The Luminous Gospels* (Telephone, TX: Praxis Publishing, 2008), 32.

[160] Pierre Teilhard de Chardin in his essay, "My Universe," written in 1924. See Pierre Teilhard de Chardin, *Science and Christ* (New York: Harper & Row, 1968), 83.

Printed in the USA
CPSIA information can be obtained
at www.ICGtesting.com
LVHW090350101023
760603LV00005B/24